Bassing

with the

Best

BASSING
WITH THE
BEST

—■—

Techniques
of America's
Top Pros

—■—

GARY WHITE

Quill
William Morrow
New York

It is the policy of William Morrow and Company, Inc., and its imprints and affiliates, recognizing the importance of preserving what has been written, to print the books we publish on acid-free paper, and we exert our best efforts to that end.

Library of Congress Cataloging-in-Publication Data

White, Gary, 1941–
Bassing with the best : techniques of America's top pros / Gary White.—1st ed.
p. cm.
ISBN 0-688-14686-4
1. Bass fishing. I. Title.
SH681.W46 1997
799.1'758—dc20   96-17992
                                                                CIP

Printed in the United States of America

First Quill Edition

5   6   7   8   9   10

BOOK DESIGN BY JENNIFER HARPER

CONTENTS

Acknowledgments

I would like to thank a few folks who helped make this book a reality.

First, I'd like to thank the pros whose techniques are high-lighted—Denny Brauer, Ken Cook, O. T. Fears, David Fritts, Robert Hamilton, Jimmy Houston, Larry Nixon, Zell Rowland, Rich Tauber, and Kevin VanDam. These individuals are professionals in every sense of the word. They share their expertise willingly and enthusiastically. Each has proven himself a "class act," both as a professional angler and as an individual who has the best interest of the sport of bass fishing at heart.

I'd also like to thank those individuals who helped accumulate the data necessary for a book of this type—Jim Morton, Ben Duncan, and Steve Nelson.

Also, thanks to my son, Gary J. White, who struggled through several rewrites and capsulized the material with his computer and writing expertise.

And finally a special thanks to the person who proofread this effort numerous times and who always offered the proper critique at the proper time. This special individual has stood by me through thick and thin and has always been my competent partner, my biggest supporter (whether I was right or wrong), and my best friend. I dedicate this effort to that special person, my wife, Mary John.

INTRODUCTION

In the past twenty years, I've worked with America's top bass pros in the Bass Fishing Techniques Institutes. During this time I've seen a trend develop. Bass fishermen in general, and the pros in particular, like to classify various lures and techniques employed to catch bass. There are many of these so-called techniques, and some of them are simply variations of other techniques. I've chosen ten of what I consider to be the most important techniques a bass fisherman can master. Concentrate on these ten and you'll find that other techniques develop as a spin-off from these.

I've also become aware that the pros love to label things. Their jargon is legend. From techniques to lures, the pros love labels. As a result the jig and pork rind bait becomes the jig and pig. The limited-line long-rod technique becomes flipping, the retrieving of a diving, wiggling lure becomes cranking, and so forth.

The bass pros, like athletes in other sports, tend to concentrate on various techniques that seem to come naturally to them. (And the bass pro is an athlete. Try standing on the front deck of a rocking bass boat, casting for eight hours a day for four straight days.) All top bass pros are competent at fishing almost any technique. However, a few have begun to excel at certain techniques so much that we've come to identify them with that particular technique. These "experts" view their special technique as their ace in the hole. They have found that they can almost always count on it to produce bass, and when conditions are just right, their special technique is a bonanza for them.

As Chris Altman, *B.A.S.S. Times* senior writer puts it, "These super-successful anglers have developed a sense, an uncanny ability to know exactly where to look for strikes. Actually these top anglers have a wealth of fishing experience accumulated over decades of trial and error and educated decisions. In the end they have amassed a knowledge base that would rival any computer database on the subject. Encouraging to most bass fishermen is the fact that these pros were not born with this fishing knowledge. Rather it is a learned skill that can be honed to a sharp talent."

The pros featured in *Bassing with the Best* are just that, the best! They are actually the *very best* at their special technique. If you emulate these pros, you will improve your bass fishing.

And just where do these special techniques work? Whether you're fishing a man-made impoundment, a natural lake, a tidal basin, moving water, or a river or tail race, these techniques will help you catch more bass. Over the years the pros have proven again and again that "a bass is a bass." A bass will almost always react the same way if the set of circumstances is the same. As a result, the pros have proven that from California to New York and from Washington, D.C., to Florida, all across America, these techniques apply. Whether you are angling for largemouth, smallmouth, or spotted bass, these techniques are applicable. However, they are most generally associated with the big brother of the black bass family, the largemouth.

The funny thing is that the black bass is really not a bass at all, but rather a member of the sunfish family. The only true freshwater bass is the white bass and its cousins, and the transplanted striped bass. The striped bass, while primarily a saltwater species, moves up freshwater rivers and streams to spawn and has been successfully transplanted to large freshwater impoundments. But, for our purposes, we are still calling the largemouth, the smallmouth, and the spotted "sunfish" a bass.

Before I introduce you to the pros that are featured in *Bassing with the Best,* let's take a quick look at their techniques, the lures they use, and how each developed.

THE JERKBAIT

The term *jerkbait* has become synonymous with the long minnow-type lures. Fishermen who employ this technique have to occasionally explain jokingly that the term *jerkbait* refers strictly to the lures and does not describe the character of the angler using it. Lures, such as the Storm Thunderstick, the Bomber Long A, and the Smithwick Rogue fall into this category.

Michigan pro Kevin VanDam and Texas pro Jay Yelas became known for "jerking" these minnow baits as they slowly retrieve the lure, thus driving the lure to its maximum depth. They would then pause and jerk the lure again. The result was a slow stop-and-start action that emulated an injured baitfish.

The technique allows an angler to draw bass up from deeper water to strike a shallow running lure. It's become one of the most effective methods for pros to cover a lot of water and fish this lure either above suspended bass or draw the fish up from the depths.

SPINNERBAITS

The name describes the lure. The early spinnerbaits were actually made from safety pins. The latch end of the pin was cut off. The sharp end was bent at a 90-degree angle and placed through the eye of the hook inside the lead mold. The head of the spinnerbait was poured over the eye of the hook with the safety pin inserted. A swivel was attached to the other end of the safety pin wire and a blade was attached to the swivel. Tie a bucktail on, or attach a rubber skirt, and you have a spinnerbait.

In the mid 1950s spinnerbaits, with a bucktail tied on the shank of the hook, began to really be noticed as a fish catcher on the new super lakes being impounded in the Southeast and the South. The old "Dragnetter" lure was a top producer on red-hot Bull Shoals, located on the Arkansas-Missouri border.

In the 1960s the basic technique was to "chunk and wind" the lures and cover as much water as possible. America's lakes and impoundments were loaded with bass and they all loved the spinnerbait!

As the pros continued to fish the spinnerbait through the late sixties and into the early seventies, they started customizing them. We saw the development of colored blades, and a variety of blade shapes, as well as new skirt designs and colors. Soon we saw "long arm" and "short arm" spinnerbaits that would fit various conditions. While the bait continues to change and evolve, the basic concept of flash and vibration as an attractant still remains. The spinnerbait may well be America's most popular lure. And why not? It will catch bass under a variety of conditions, it covers a lot of water, and it allows you to present your lure to as many bass as possible.

PLASTIC WORMS

The first commercial plastic worms impacted the market right after World War II. Nick Creme's fake wiggler, called the Scoundrel, was one of the first. These lures were originally rigged with multiple single hooks inserted into the lure and tied together with monofilament line. At the head of the worm several beads were strung on the monofilament and a propeller added. As crude as the lure sounds, it will still catch fish today.

As the new "Texas rig" became popular in the 1960s, anglers learned that this technique would allow them to fish in places that other lures could not go. With the hook embedded in the worm, the lure could swim and penetrate brush piles, rocks, and cover that would snag an exposed hook almost immediately. The result was many more strikes from larger bass. The problem became how to set the hook. Early plastic-worm anglers soon learned that they needed stiffer rods and heavier line to set the hook and move bass from heavy cover.

Early plastic worm hook setting was almost comical. The first approach I can remember was to let the bass run with the lure until he stopped. Then you would set the hook hard. Of course, in many cases the fish had circled several underwater obstacles and at times had actually doubled back under the boat. Imagine the surprise when an angler set the hook only to have the bass jump on the opposite side of the boat.

The plastic worm technique lets an angler fish at a variety of depths, from the shallows to deep drop-offs, with a lifelike lure that is almost snagproof.

FLIPPING AND PITCHING

Dee Thomas, a California angler, has been called by many the Father of Flipping. After experimenting with a 12-foot-long rod, Thomas finally settled on a 7½-foot saltwater rod and began to swing underhanded casts with a heavy jig. The technique enabled him to penetrate cover and handle big bass on the heavy line and long stiff rod. Thomas introduced his technique, which he called flipping, on the B.A.S.S. tour in the mid seventies, and its popularity zoomed.

In the 1980s, Denny Brauer and Tommy Biffle began to employ a version of flipping that became known as pitching.

This "long-distance flip" expanded the limited-line casts of flipping by releasing the free spool reel and thrusting the lure forward with the same underhanded cast used in flipping. However, the weight of the lure (usually a jig) allowed the line to free-spool off the reel and the lure to be carried a greater distance. This enabled anglers to spook fewer fish since they were not not as close to their target.

When bass are inactive, for a variety of reasons (heavy fishing pressure, passage of a cold front, high sunny skies, etc.), flipping and pitching allows an angler to penetrate the dense cover where bass will hold under these conditions. It's a mainstay in the arsenal of most pros.

TOPWATER

The topwater technique has been termed the greatest thrill in bass fishing. Truly nothing matches a surging topwater strike. Topwater lures date back to the dawn of bass fishing. In the early 1900s anglers were carving topwater lures and attaching treble hooks. Anglers learned that topwater disturbances could attract a bass's attention. These handmade lures gave way to the early manufactured topwater lures such as the Arbogast Hula Popper and the forerunner of the buzzbait, the Hawaiian Wiggler.

As other lures and techniques developed, with the bass-fishing explosion of the sixties and seventies, topwater began to take a backseat. Topwater techniques required that anglers impart action to the lure. And it did require practice to be able to make these baits walk, chug, pop, and dart. Anglers became interested in lures that provided their own action. However, pros like Zell Rowland and Charlie Campbell held firm to the virtues of topwater and proved time and again that in the hands of an expert these "old-timers" are very effective and just as much fun as ever. These pros have also refined the technique in regard to using topwater for schooling fish and to attract bass in deeper water off points and midlake structure.

CRANKBAITS

The crankbait is the latest terminology for what old-timers referred to as plugs. These lures, made of wood or plastic, have their own built-in action. All you need to do is cast them out and crank them back. Thus the term *crankbait*. Others have referred to these lures as idiot baits, since it was said that anyone could catch fish on them.

The crankbait craze was launched in the early 1970s with the creation of the Big O. This handmade lure, designed and built by Fred Young of Tennessee, looked more like an egg than a baitfish. The pregnant minnow, as it was termed, proved to be a tremendous fish catcher. The pros hoarded these handmade gems. With their newly developed trolling motors they could move rapidly down a shoreline and crank these lures over a tremendously wide area, prospecting for bass with every cast.

The Big O was bought out by the Cordell Lure Co., and soon other lure manufacturers followed with their versions. We began to see Big Ns, Big As, Fat Alberts, and every variation imaginable. The industry has continued to crank out new crankbaits of all sizes and shapes each year to satisfy a seemingly endless need.

Within the last few years crankbaits with larger diving bills have taken center stage. The pros quickly adopted these new, deeper divers, and pros like David Fritts, Mark Davis, and Mike Auten began to locate bass away from the shoreline on humps, creek, channels, and underwater structure. Using lighter lines and softer rods to keep from tearing treble hooks from the bass's mouth, this new deep-water cranking brought a whole new technique into the crankbait picture.

TUBE-BAIT FINESSE

With the development of so many lures and techniques during the sixties and seventies the fishing pressure in certain areas became extreme. Bass began to react to smaller, more subtle lures. Western anglers developed a technique and system that became known as finesse fishing. It utilized smaller lures, lighter lines, and scaled-down rods and reels. These were more suited to the deep, clear, rocky western lakes. As the technique was exported from the West and made its appearance on the B.A.S.S. circuit, the old pros referred to the finesse lures as sissy baits. However, it quickly became obvious that these "sissy baits" belonged in the tackle box of every serious bass angler.

The tube bait and its technique is what we will be highlighting. This tiny bait resembles a miniature squid and was originally designed in Utah by Bobby Garland. It was called a Gitzit, and as with other successful lures, imitations followed immediately.

In the 1980s the popularity of the tube bait hits its zenith. California bass pro Rich Tauber parlayed his skill with the tiny bait into a fifty-thousand-dollar check by winning the U.S. Open Bass Tournament. The bait can be fished on either a jig head or the super-weedless "Gitzit Glider." Each employs a slightly different technique, but either way it is a change of pace that bass find irresistible.

CAROLINA RIG

The Carolina rig is a variation of the Do Nothin' worm rig, and some say predated it. The rig and technique was developed in the Carolinas as far back as the 1970s, but didn't catch the public's attention until the 1980s. As is almost always the case, the bass pro picks up on a technique, which then leads the weekend basser to it. Such is the case with the Carolina rig.

The pros began to utilize this technique to "hunt" bass over a large area. It can be fished at almost any depth effectively by varying the size of the slip sinker.

Oklahoma pro O. T. Fears broke two existing B.A.S.S. records in 1994 by using the Carolina-rig method. For a three-day B.A.S.S. event (five-bass limit) he caught a record 77 pounds 4 ounces of bass. He also set a new one-day (five-bass limit) record of 34 pounds 4 ounces.

The rig is simple—a slip-sinker weight ahead of a bead strung on your line. A barrel swivel is then attached. To the swivel you tie a leader of varying lengths from line usually testing less than the main line. To this is tied a plastic-worm hook of your choice. Any number of soft plastic lures can be fished on this rig, but the number-one choice is the plastic lizard.

For casting points, paralleling creek channels, or mining offshore structure, the versatile Carolina rig has established its place among the techniques effective anglers need to employ.

THE SLUGGO-TYPE LURE

Every now and then a lure and technique comes along that has virtually no predecessor. Most lures and techniques have been developed and refined over a period of decades. The Sluggo-type plastic lure is an exception to the rule. Designed and developed by Herb Reed, a graphic artist from Connecticut, the Sluggo was intended as a smallmouth bass lure. Developed for Reed's own use, the Sluggo looks more like a garden slug than a fishing lure, but oh how it catches bass! Every species—smallmouth, largemouth, and spotted bass—seem to love this ugly creation.

From those first 1987 hand-poured Sluggo lures sprang Lunker City Lures.

Herb Reed now produces the Sluggo and several other effective lures for the bassin' masses. Other companies brought out their own version—Mister Twister's Slimy Slug, Kalin's Hop-a-Long, and Mann Bait Co.'s Shadow, to name a few. However, the term *Sluggo* has stuck to this type of lure, much as consumers use the term *Kleenex* to describe all brands of tissue.

The technique is, for the most part, effective in mainly shallow water. The erratic action of a Sluggo is something entirely different from other soft plastic lures. This Johnny-come-lately lure and technique has earned a spot in our top ten.

BASS BEHAVIOR

This is not a special lure or tactic, but it may be the most important topic of all. The bass-fishing public is always searching for that secret lure—the one that will catch bass every day, under any set of circumstances. This search is what keeps the lure companies cranking out new and improved versions year after year. It's the reason why many of us have three hundred lures in our tackle box, when it only takes one to catch a bass.

The pros know what this secret is and it is not a lure at all. It is knowledge of bass behavior. How bass react to color, scent, pH, and oxygen. How they move and spawn and relocate. Knowledge of these factors can multiply your effectiveness many times over.

Ken Cook is a professional bass angler and one of the best. He is also a scientist and has spent years studying bass behavior. When Ken Cook talks about bass behavior, even the pros listen. So take it to heart when Ken teaches about why bass do what they do. It could improve your effectiveness more than any technique.

Now that we've touched on our top ten topics, let's get with it! Let's go *Bassing with the Best*.

BASSING

WITH THE

BEST

Ken Cook—a scientist and a top professional angler—
shares his insight into bass behavior.

1

WHY BASS DO
WHAT THEY DO

Unraveling Bass Biology with Ken Cook

Ken Cook grew up in the roll-ing hills of eastern Okla-homa, and his passion for fishing started early. Even today he likes to reminisce about those early years when he rattled down dusty roads on his bicycle, a tough old fiberglass rod and Zebco spincast reel across the handlebars, the fat front tire bouncing over big chunks of gravel as he raced the summer sun to a shady spot beside some nearby creek or pond.

Fishing and hunting were the focus of young Ken's life, and as he grew older, he decided to con-centrate on making his avocation and vocation merge into one. By the time Cook was in high school, eastern Oklahoma's rivers were be-ing dammed one after another by an ambitious U.S. Army Corps of

KEN COOK
MEERS, OKLAHOMA

1991 BASS Masters Classic Champion. U.S. Open and Super Bass Winner. Twelve-time BASS Masters Classic Finalist. Holds a college degree in Wildlife Biology.

Engineers construction program that produced thousands of acres of new fishing waters. One reservoir in particular, Lake Eufaula, was near Ken's hometown. Soon after it filled, Eufaula proved to be a bass-fishing bonanza, and Cook was there as often as he could be to cash in.

The Eufaula experience was like a compass for the young outdoorsman. He saw the potential of bass fishing, the excitement it stirred, the following it attracted. So Cook decided to make fishing his life in the most literal of terms. The country boy became a collegian and earned an ambitious prize: a degree in Wildlife Biology. A few years later professional biologist Ken Cook was a member of the Oklahoma Department of Wildlife Conservation Fisheries Team, where he earned a living surveying, stocking, and managing the sport-fish populations of many of the lakes he'd dreamed about as a fuzzy-cheeked youngster. Still, he couldn't forget how much he loved just plain fishing, and how much the need to outsmart *Micropterus salmoides* still haunted him. However, his duties as a wildlife biologist were teaching him valuable lessons about bass behavior.

LEARNING FIRSTHAND

Ken recalls one instance that has stayed with him to this day. He was on a scale-sample study on a local lake. In this study the biologists use a "shocking boat," a craft fitted with a device that sends an electric shock into the water. This shock stuns fish in close proximity for a few minutes. They float up, and are netted by the biologist, who carefully takes a few scales off the fish, then returns them to the lake unharmed. By studying the scales, growth rates can be determined. On this particular day several anglers were fishing in the area where the survey was being taken. The biologist waited patiently for the anglers to fish the area thoroughly. After they had all moved on without so much as a strike, the biologists eased in for their study effort. Their shocking survey found the area to be teeming with keeper-size bass. The anglers had given up too soon. Ken calls this situation to mind when he is in a promising area that is not producing. Many times he will remain in the area and keep changing tactics. At other times he will leave the area and return later in the day. Ken's experience as a biologist has taught him where bass hold and how they move and relocate during the seasons.

LIFE-CHANGING EVENTS

When the Wildlife Department assigned Cook to their regional office near Lawton, Oklahoma, the biologist decided to join a bass-fishing group and test his competitive skills. Cook quickly found out that tournament fishing was tough. On the other hand, each trial offered a new and different set of tests to challenge both his scientific knowledge and physical skills. Soon Ken was winning local and regional amateur tournaments, then B.A.S.S. events. Winning the $100,000 first-place money in the first Super B.A.S.S. Tournament in 1981 was all the impetus Cook needed to quit his job as a biologist and take to the water as a full-time professional fisherman. "This was an unforgettable moment for me," Cook remembers. "The Super B.A.S.S. Tournament changed my life by allowing me to concentrate full-time on bass fishing." Ken quickly became a force in the pro bass field and went on to win the B.A.S.S. Masters Classic. Today he's a respected angler who combines savvy and science to remain one of America's top-rated bass experts.

Here, then, is Ken Cook on both the science and the skills of bass fishing. The following was compiled from a series of interviews with Ken, plus a number of informal conversations we've had from time to time.

BLACK BASS: A SPECIES ANALYSIS

Let's begin with the basics. There are three main species of black bass in North America: largemouth bass, smallmouth bass, and spotted bass (Illustration 1.1). The largemouth is generally the largest fish overall. It also has the biggest mouth, thus the name. Largemouth bass prefer calm, shallow water with plenty of concealing cover, such as weeds, submerged logs, or maybe rocky ledges. The largemouth is the slowest of the three and prefers to hug close to cover in most cases.

Smallmouth bass are less confined than largemouths to submerged cover such as stumps, trees, or grass beds. Smallmouths will also roam away from cover or underwater structure and wander deeper than largemouth bass. If any sort of current exists, then smallmouth bass are more likely to orient themselves to it. Smallmouth prefer gravel and rocks as cover.

Spotted bass are intermediate between largemouth and smallmouth bass. They tend to live deeper than the other two species and spawn in deeper waters. However, spotted bass rarely grow as large as either largemouths or smallmouths.

Due to the physical characteristics of these fish, spotted and smallmouth bass are usually caught on smaller or more finesse-type baits, while the largemouth, due to its greater mouth size, will select larger prey. That's why you can catch them on larger baits.

We've mentioned that largemouth bass prefer lots of cover. They can also tolerate more turbidity and less water quality than their cousins. Smallmouth bass need high-quality, clear waters. Largemouths may do okay in a lake or stream that's nutrient-rich and contains a high level of microscopic plankton, while smallmouths seek cleaner water and a current if available.

Once again, spotted bass sort of slide into the niche between these two. They can be found in or around a current,

Illustration 1.1

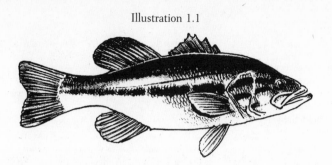

Largemouth: *America's favorite gamefish, the largemouth is found in every state of the continental United States and in Hawaii. The largemouth has been known to dine on shad, frogs, crawfish, bluegills, and even small mammals and birds.*

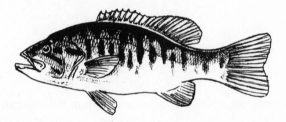

Smallmouth: *The smallmouth has been described as "ounce for ounce, the gamest fish that swims." Its food preference is crawfish, minnows, and shad.*

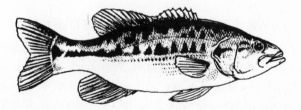

Spotted Bass: *For many years it was thought to be a cross between the largemouth and smallmouth bass. We now know that the "spot" is a separate entity in the black bass family. Like the smallmouth, the spotted bass prefers crawfish, minnows, and shad.*

continued

	COLOR	MARKINGS	BODY CHARACTERISTICS
LARGEMOUTH	Dark green on the back and almost white on the belly, the color gradually becoming lighter from back to belly.	Has a well-defined stripe running the length of its body.	Its upper jaw extends past the bass's eye. Does not have a patch of teeth on tongue.
SMALLMOUTH	Its brownish gold color has earned it the nickname brownie, brown bass, or bronzeback.	Has nine dark vertical bars on the side of the body.	Its upper jaw extends to the middle of the eye. Has a patch of teeth on tongue.
SPOTTED BASS	Bright green and sometimes turquoise back.	Well-defined markings consist of dark horizontal bands on each side broken into diamond shapes.	The mouth size is between that of a largemouth and a smallmouth. Has a patch of teeth on tongue.

less so than smallmouths, yet more so than largemouths. Their water-quality demands fall right in the middle between largemouths and smallmouths, yet they can be found associating with both. You also need to remember there are several species of spotted bass that have adapted to specialized niches within these habitat requirements.

LINK LURES TO FAVORED FOODS

Cook's personal approach to catching these fish is based on differences in their food habits. Largemouth bass will eat just about anything they can see and swallow, from crawfish up to larger shad. In fact crawfish may be the common denominator in the food chain for all three species—they all prefer them.

So if Ken is fishing for largemouth bass and using a crawfish imitator, he'll tie on a larger bait, such as a big jig or a big crankbait. If he's fishing for smallmouth bass, then he'll switch to something with a smaller profile, such as a hair jig or a twin tail grub. Generally, he'll fish with smaller baits for smallmouth and spotted bass. He'll also fish deeper, because you usually catch smallmouth and spotted bass at greater depths than large-mouths. This has a lot to do with water quality, since small-mouths and spots need clearer water, and clear water means the fish will be deeper. So it all comes back to habitat.

THE OXYGEN FACTOR

There's also the matter of oxygen. Fish need oxygen to breathe and metabolize food, just as we do. Oxygen is present in the water due to photosynthesis by green plants or tiny particles of plankton.

Water with a high oxygen content does not necessarily mean that bass will congregate there. On the other hand, the pH, or acidity, factor often serves as a much better indicator of where good fishing may be found.

pH: BASS CHEMISTRY THAT'S TOO OFTEN OVERLOOKED

Basically pH is a measure of the relative amount of hydrogen ions in water, which determines whether it is acid or alkaline. Measurements are based on a scale of 0 to 14, with 7 being neutral. Actually it's a logarithm scale, meaning that if you move from 7 to 8, you've changed by a factor of 10 the proportion of hydrogen ions.

So when you reach the end of the scale, there can be a big difference in the water's pH. This is important, since bass have a pH range in which they function most efficiently. They don't actually prefer a certain pH factor; however, their metabolism is most efficient when the pH of the water is close to the pH factor of their blood, which is 7.4.

When all other factors are equal, bass are most active at

pH levels between 7 and 9. Take them out of that range and the fish find it difficult to retrieve oxygen from the water and transport it through their gill capillaries into their bloodstream. The pH factor is not as easily measured as the temperature or color of the water, yet it is extremely important in determining how the bass actually feel—if you have difficulty breathing, you're not as active as you are when your respiratory system is functioning perfectly and you feel at the peak of health.

The pH factor is determined by rainfall and by photosynthesis, the metabolic process of green plants. Rainfall tends to increase the water's acidity, which brings the pH down to the lower end of the scale. Generally, rainfall has a pH factor of about 5.2 or 5.3. In some places it is even much lower than that, yet rarely will it ever be higher.

Therefore rainfall runoff entering a lake, unless it is buffered by something like limestone, can lower the pH values of a lake. This is particularly true in the spring, because in most cases the water is still cold, plants in the lake remain dormant, and very little photosynthesis is taking place. Factors that raise pH levels are mostly missing in winter and early spring.

When you're looking for bass, you should be looking for water with a pH rating in that heightened productivity range of 7 to 9. Generally pH levels in the spring are going to decline as you go deeper due to lack of photosynthesis. In summer, plants are growing and there is usually less rainfall, so pH factors are high. On the opposite end of the spectrum, when these same plants die back and decay, the decomposition process uses up oxygen in the water and the pH levels are once again low.

It's all part of the natural life-and-death cycle of living waters. If plants receive sunlight, they grow and raise the pH factor. If they are deprived of sunlight, plants die back and pH values are lowered. Obviously, pH will be higher at the surface, lower at the bottom. Often in the summer, particularly in fertile water, there will be a period when photosynthesis is occurring at a rapid rate and establishes a sort of breakline at a certain depth where pH values change rapidly. This will be a key zone for bass.

PH AND THE THERMOCLINE

In warm weather, if there is a thermocline, or stratified layer of warm over cold water, you'll often find the pH break associated with it. If there's no thermocline, then the pH breakline—if there is one—may be limited by turbidity or by the plants themselves. If you run into an extremely fertile situation where there is a lot of plankton in the water, the plankton will cut off the amount of sunlight entering the water and the breakline may be only a few feet in depth.

Sometimes you'll encounter a pH break that occurs along a line where plants stop growing and start dying. These fertile situations create a zone that sponsors a shallow-pitch breakline, and it will remain shallow even though the water becomes very hot in the summertime.

TEST pH FOR A PROVEN ADVANTAGE

As you can see, fishermen who know how to use a pH meter have a big advantage. In springtime, the best way to use the meter is through a series of surface readings, exploring horizontally to find areas with the best rates. In summer, you'll probably be fishing the main body of the lake, so take readings at various depths, searching for that breakline we've discussed, because that's where fish will congregate.

At times you can find both the pH breakline and the thermocline with the aid of the depth finder on your boat. Turn the sensitivity level up as high as it will go and then just drive around the lake, noting the depth where you see fish. Sometimes you'll also see the breakline and thermocline due to the abrupt change in the density of the water. There will be a layer of microscopic plants and plankton that have died and sunk toward the bottom, only to be held in suspension on the thermocline. This will show up as a line on your depth finder. Plus you need to note that schools of baitfish never seem to go beyond a certain depth—that in itself should tell you how deep you need to fish.

In summertime situations, your depth finder can do an adequate job of helping you locate the pH breakline. The most important thing is understanding why you should be fishing at that depth. In the summer, pH is mostly influenced by photosynthesis. Sunlight is the key to photosynthesis, so there can be a drastic daily change in pH values between night and day. Factors fall off rather spectacularly at night in fertile waters, and then climb right back up during the day. This explains why fishing can be so good in shallow water at night and then be so bad in the same shallows when the summer sun climbs in the sky. The pH factor just gets too high.

BASS AND THE ABILITY TO SEE COLOR

Anglers also need to remember that bass have extremely acute color vision. When fish grow accustomed to feeding on certain prey, such as crawfish in the spring, they develop a tendency to key in on anything that's the color of a crawfish. Naturally, it would be an advantage to match these colors with your lure.

Overall visibility is another factor. Bass are naturally curious and opportunistic, and they will often attack something that appears abnormal. That's why bright lure colors draw strikes, even though they may not resemble anything natural in the animal's environment. If the water is clear and the fish have a relatively long sight distance, use more natural colors, including crawfish, shad, or bluegill patterns. On the other hand, if the water is muddy or the fish are in heavy cover, such as grass beds, then I turn to the higher-visibility colors, such as chartreuse, red, blue, or orange.

BASS AND THE SENSE OF SMELL

Bass also have a highly developed olfactory system. They can detect a small amount of chemicals in the water and then assess whether or not these chemicals are advantageous to their well-being. Fish use scent to investigate their environment. They probably don't swim around using their noses to find food. However, bass use scent to unravel clues that pertain to what's happening in their surroundings.

Scent can enhance your fishing, if you use it properly. Negative scents, of course, produce just the opposite effect. The use of a good manufactured scent can cause bass to cue to a bait in a positive manner. Scents aren't magical, but they are a tool that can be used to the angler's advantage.

BASS AND WATER TEMPERATURE

Now let's move on to water temperature. Bass are cold-blooded, therefore their metabolism rate goes up as the water temperature climbs. Water temperature may be the most important factor in the bass environment. It is key to how they feel, how well they metabolize food, and thus how easy they are to catch.

A bass that is metabolizing, or using its food, efficiently is an opportunistic predator. Bass are generally at their physical peak in waters that range between 65 and 85 degrees. Outside that range, bass tend to be less aggressive, or less normal. Any substandard environmental factors—high pH, low pH, water too hot or too cold—will cause these fish to become somewhat less than an opportunistic predator and therefore more difficult to catch.

Good fishermen take all of these water factors into consideration. They measure pH, oxygen content, and temperature. These readings will tell them how and where to fish. If you're fishing cold water, say around 50 degrees, then it's predetermined that bass are not going to be very aggressive. This is when good anglers slow down their presentations and turn to smaller baits. As conditions improve, your chances are going to improve at the same rate.

BASS AND THE SPRING SPAWN

Every spring, when the water temperature edges into the 60-degree range, there comes a period of biological renewal that bass fishermen anticipate with near reverence. We refer to this breeding season as the spawn, and it's the time when male bass move into shallow water as the days grow longer and the water warmer.

Smallmouth and spotted bass spawn in a little bit deeper water and at slightly cooler temperatures than largemouth bass. However, in this case I'm going to concentrate on the largemouth spawn, because that's the fish that the majority of bass anglers are concerned with.

As the hours of daylight grow longer in early spring, bass instinctively move to shallow water. When water temperatures reach that magic 60-degree mark, male fish begin searching for a suitable nesting site.

The bass seek a spot that consists of a relatively hard bottom with no silt, maybe over sand or rocks or underwater roots. After the site has been chosen, the males fan out a nest with their tails, cleaning the area as thoroughly as possible.

Once the spawning site has been established, the females arrive, and the males begin the process of attracting them to the nest they've prepared. A single male will attract several females to his nest over a period of time. The female deposits a

Illustration 1.2 *After fanning a spot for the nest, the male bass herds a female onto the nest to deposit her eggs. After fertilization, the male bass stands guard until the fry are hatched.*

few eggs while the male fertilizes them, then later the male repeats the process with another female (Illustration 1.2).

Each female will release some of her eggs into the nests of several males. This is nature's way of ensuring a broad genetic mix. It also helps prolong the spawning season a bit, a factor that enhances the chances of a successful spawn in any given year.

It takes bass eggs only three days to hatch in 60-degree

water, so a complete spawn can happen fast. Females visit nests one at a time over a period of three days, then eggs start to hatch and suddenly the male has a swarm of hatchling bass, called fry, to guard. Males watch the fry for a day or so and then return to their normal routine. Generally, at the end of the spawn, adult fish return to deeper water.

However, we shouldn't oversimplify something as crucial as the spawning season. For one thing, any given female may not spawn all her eggs in one week, or even in one month. I believe that in many cases, females tend to cycle through a couple of reproductive periods. I don't mean that they make new eggs throughout the season, only that their ovaries aren't completely emptied during a single spawning urge.

Maybe there will be spawning activity that begins under an early-spring full moon, then a cold front sweeps down, and the bass either slow down the spawning process or back off completely. Then, twenty-eight days later, under the peak of another full moon, the spawn will commence again, and this time it will be much more vigorous and successful.

So it actually takes a six- to eight-week period to complete a spawn, with some fish on a nest and some off during the entire time frame. Once again, this is nature's way of guaranteeing that a single bad weather event doesn't destroy an entire spawning season. The best way to avoid catastrophe is to spread the spawn out over several weeks' time and among several different individual fish.

FISHING THE SPAWN

For bass fishermen, there are three key periods associated with the spawn, and each should be approached differently to achieve maximum angling success. The first is the prespawn period, when the water temperature is in the 50s and bass are moving into shallow water, searching for food and preparing to spawn.

During prespawn it's essential for fish to eat as much and as often as possible, which they'll do as long as the water is growing warmer. Then, when a cold front blasts down from the north, the water temperature drops, metabolism levels drop, feeding slows down, and bass are content to hang back with their stomachs full and wait for a warming trend. Obviously, fishing then can be tough.

Then the weather gets better, the water grows warmer and the bass grow active once more. Their metabolism rates are racing and they're on the prowl for something—anything—to eat. The fish need to build up fat and energy reserves for the upcoming spawn, they're feeding voraciously, and fishing is excellent.

When bass enter the actual spawning season, they show a tendency to disregard food, since the reproductive urge is much more critical. At this time they are more territorial than hungry. During the prespawn, Ken's number-one choice of baits is some sort of crawfish imitation. When the fish first begin moving into shallow water, he'll go with a jig or a crawfish-colored crankbait. Later, when the fish are coming into the spawn and the water temperature nears 60 degrees, spinnerbaits become a factor. At this time it's best to throw a little bit bigger bait, because the fish are seeking prey that are a little bit larger.

During the actual spawning season many successful bass fishermen turn to territorial-infringement baits; lures in bright colors, jerkbaits, tube baits, lizards. These are baits that fish see in their spawning territory and immediately attack. This natural biological reaction is the reason why so many fish are caught during the spawn.

Postspawn is a tough time for most bass anglers. One of the

Illustration 1.3 *Depending on water temperature and frontal passages, bass will move toward the shallows in early spring. Before they move to the spawning areas they will hold or "stage," usually at the first drop to deeper water.*

reasons is that when bass move, they move a lot. As we've already discussed, the spawn is a process that continues over a period of weeks. Fish are constantly on and off spawning beds, and as the spawn winds down, a lot of bass are in the process of relocating.

Many move offshore, remain suspended in the water, and are actually in a feeding mode. Their metabolism is high and they are definitely looking for something to eat. However, fishing for them can be tough simply because many of us have a hard time locating these fish (Illustration 1.3).

Sometimes these bass move out from the shoreline and suspend for hours during the day. Then, when they begin to move and look for something to eat, the fish will be easy to catch. Mostly, anglers seem to be stymied because the bass aren't where they've been accustomed to finding them—the fishermen just lose track of the fish. Generally, postspawn feeding is more in the summer mode for bass, when their appetites turn to bluegill and shad. This is why it's advantageous to use typical summer baits: sunfish and shad-colored crankbaits, plastic worms, spinnerbaits.

ANGLING BY THE CALENDAR: ESTABLISHING SEASONAL PATTERNS FOR BASS

Good anglers pay attention to seasonal patterns. If you keep a logbook on your fishing activities, it becomes clear that fish are caught in different parts of the lake in different times of the year. In the winter, bass migrate to the main body of the lake, and you'll find them where it's deeper, steeper, and clearer in most cases. They won't move much, and the fish prefer to hold tight against steep structure, such as bluffs, because this provides quick and easy access to shallow water.

In the spring, bass move into the shallows for food and in preparation for the spawn. Therefore, springtime fishing is generally associated with coves and smaller creek channels. Due to negative pH factors fish don't move up into creeks with a lot of heavy runoff. Ken fishes coves without a creek channel because of the better water quality. Bass move shallow and this is a super-productive time. Many anglers catch a few and return there in the summer and in the fall, expecting similar action. This generally does not produce, since the spring bass have moved on to other seasonal haunts.

In the summertime, bass move back to the main body of the lake. Fish may not move great distances, measured in miles, out of some cove and back to bigger water, but they certainly do move. Summer fishing patterns are usually associated with the main lake or midlake structure, or long points that extend out into the main lake.

Summertime structure fishing involves convex structure, or

keying in on objects that stick up from the bottom of the lake. In winter, the pattern's just the opposite: you should look for concave structure, such as underwater channel banks that are situated deep on the inside of an abrupt drop-off.

In the summer, bass show a tendency to locate on a hump or a point, something that sticks up above the bottom. In the fall, bass are most often found wherever schools of shad can be found, such as the upper stretches of a creek that enters the lake.

Autumn is a time when you actually want to fish creeks that have rainfall runoff. Runoff brings down nutrients that enhance the plankton base that shad feed on. Therefore shad migrate into these creek channels, and the bass follow them to some degree. So fall patterns should key in on creeks, rivers, and the upper portions of the lake.

Bait patterns should correspond to what the fish are eating during a particular time of the year. In winter this would be small minnows and shad. In the spring it's crayfish. After the spawn, it's sunfish and shad. Following the midsummer shad spawn, 90 percent of the bass's diet in most reservoirs is shad.

KEYING IN ON THE EDGE EFFECT

You should also remember that bass are extremely edge oriented. The two main edges of a lake are the bottom and the top. Other important edges include channels, grasslines, treelines, an old flooded fencerow, or any kind of dropoff. Anytime you find a junction of two edges, there's a high percentage that bass will be there. In fact the fish show a tendency to "stack up" in such places, so edges are truly important to good bass fishing.

SKIPPING OVER UNPRODUCTIVE WATER

When you decide to eliminate unproductive water in a lake, start with water-quality tools, such as temperature gauges and pH meters. What you're generally looking for is fertility—water that's not muddy, yet stained by a lot of plankton. Plankton is the base of the food chain, and if there's a lot of plankton, there's a lot of shad, and therefore a lot of bass.

Generally, bass-fishing success hinges on a few simple rules. In the winter, dress warmly and fish deep. In the spring, go early in the morning, fish shallow, and plan to stay late. In the summer, get off the bank, get out into the main body of the lake, locate underwater structure, turn on your sonar system, and search for fish holding onto structure. Use your electronic tools and learn how to interpret what they're telling you. In the fall, follow the baitfish into the upper creek channels. Do that, and you'll begin to catch bass.

With all we have learned about bass behavior, Cook believes that we have only scratched the surface. He feels that there are a lot of holes in the knowledge and that other beliefs are largely unproven. In the future, biologists will be investigating in depth how a bass's senses work. He also thinks that how bass hear as compared with how we conceptualize it now will see some great advancement.

The Oklahoma pro feels that perhaps the one thing that bass fishermen need to develop above all else is open-mindedness. The ability to observe and be aware is probably the biggest key to learning from your surroundings. Cook feels that this has been a major factor in his success as a bass angler.

Kevin VanDam, possibly the most successful pro of the 1990s, has utilized jerkbaits to win two national bass fishing titles.

2

KEVIN VANDAM

He Loves to Fish Those Jerkbaits

When a major fishing-tackle manufacturer agrees to sponsor an up-and-coming bass pro, they cross their fingers and hope that he rises to their expectation level. Many of these newcomers shine brightly for a short while and then disappear from atop the standings as quickly as they arrived. Those companies who took a chance on this rising young star back in 1991 are not sorry today. Since he arrived on the scene, all Kevin has done is win the B.A.S.S. Angler of the Year award, not once but twice, 1992 and 1996. This honor is awarded to the angler who finishes first in the overall B.A.S.S. standings, at the end of each year's tournament trail. Needless to say, this is a very impressive accomplishment.

KEVIN VANDAM
KALAMAZOO, MICHIGAN

He has won the coveted B.A.S.S. Angler of the Year twice, in 1992 and 1996, in just six years on the pro tour. Six-time BASS Masters Classic Finalist.

Beginning in 1991, his rookie year, he has qualified for the BASS Masters Classic every year and has won two national bass fishing titles. Not bad for a northerner, from Michigan, adrift in a sea of good ole southern boys. Many of his fellow pros have forgiven him for talking funny, and now seek his advice on various techniques.

EARLY DAYS AND A DESIRE TO COMPETE

Kevin VanDam grew up in Michigan, where his dad and brother took him fishing for all kinds of species. They fished natural lakes, rivers, and the Great Lakes whenever possible. When he was sixteen, and got his driver's license, he followed the different runs and spawns, fishing for everything from crappie to salmon. He read every outdoor magazine he could get his hands on, but *Bassmaster* was his favorite. As he began to concentrate his fishing efforts more and more on black bass, he wondered if he could really compete on a national level. Kevin took the big step in 1991, at twenty-three years of age, encouraged by his father. Ever since then he has been a major force in professional angling. Since VanDam took top honors in the Michigan B.A.S.S. Top 100 Tournament, using a jerkbait almost exclusively, he has become a primary spokesman for the technique.

Kevin remembers, "Back in 1991, when I fished with the pros that first year, my goal was not to become a professional angler. I just wanted to see if I could compete with the top guys I'd read about and seen on TV. I'd always looked up to them. I really didn't know if I would succeed or not."

WHAT IS A JERKBAIT?

VanDam explains that the jerkbait is not one particular lure but a category of different lures. The Michigan pro classifies jerkbaits as long minnow-type baits, such as the Smithwick Rogue, the Bomber Long A, the Storm Thunderstick, and the Rapala. Each lure has a slightly different action, but each is a shallow runner.

VanDam points out that under the right circumstances the jerkbait is an absolute killer. He says that for it to be really effective, you need to have clear enough water for good visibility and you have to have bass in that depth zone where they can actually see the lure. "When these combinations come together," Kevin says, "the jerkbait can be an awesome lure." He likens its action to that of a wounded or dying fish, with a real erratic presentation, and says the bait does lots of different things. "It will entice bass in the area that are not even active," claims VanDam. "Depending on the color you select, the lure can emulate everything from a shad to a shiner to a blue-gill."

SELECT LURE COLOR
AIMED AT VISIBILITY

The two-time B.A.S.S. Angler of the Year feels that jerkbait color is very important. He chooses a color based on its visibility, trying to make the lure as visible as possible for the water and sky conditions that exist on that particular day. For instance, if it is really bright and sunny, then VanDam likes flashy colors, such as chrome, silver, and gold. He feels that these can be seen by the bass from a greater distance. "That's the key," states VanDam. "Getting the bass to see the lure from as far away as possible, and still keep some resemblance to a natural baitfish. On the other hand, when it's cloudy," VanDam points out, "you don't get a lot of flash off a chrome or gold bait." At those times, he tends to choose a chartreuse or pearl-colored lure. If the water is stained or dingy, where you have only two feet of clarity, then he uses a bright orange or other bright colors.

LURE SIZE IS IMPORTANT

The Michigan pro states that he primarily uses 4½- or 5½-inch lures. Kevin has tried them all, and he personally has about four hundred in his tackle box, but this length of lure is his favorite. He also says that different brands of baits do different things. Some have variations in the bill, so they dive shallower or deeper. Kevin's favorite jerkbait is the Smithwick Rattlin' Rogue, but he says all are effective at times.

BASIC EQUIPMENT FOR THE JERKBAIT TECHNIQUES

VanDam prefers to pick a rod that has a tapered tip, usually in the medium- to medium-light-action range. He prefers a graphite rod because he feels it gives the lure more action. As a rule of thumb, he says to select a rod about the same height as the caster is tall. "I'm six feet tall and I use a six-foot casting rod with a pistol-grip handle," states VanDam. "I use either a spinning or a casting rod, and prefer this type of action and length in both.

"I use a high-speed-retrieve reel because I never pull the lure toward the boat with the reel. I always jerk the rod tip down and pick up the slack with my reel. A fast reel picks up slack quicker."

Kevin also feels that line size is critical. He prefers line that is abrasive resistant and has low stretch. Kevin continues, "These types of lines hold up real well with this technique. Primarily, I use 8-, 10-, and 12-pound test, and tie directly to the lure. I do not use a snap." Kevin will also use line size to control the depth the lure runs. He goes up to 17- or even 20-pound test if he's fishing over vegetation. He points out that if a jerkbait is worked on a 20-pound test line, it will only run half as deep. Likewise, if the lure is on 6-pound test, he can get an extra foot or so of depth out of the lure because the diameter of the line is smaller.

THE RETRIEVE AND STRIKE

Kevin VanDam's most valuable piece of advice to anglers who fish the jerkbait technique is to learn the correct retrieve. "It's a jerk-stop thing and I try not to get into any kind of rhythm," he explains. "Some guys say jerk the lure twice and let it stop. I say twitch it two or three times and let it stop, then twitch it once, twice, or three times in random order." VanDam feels that the retrieve is what brings the lure to life. He also feels that it is the difference between catching a few or a livewell full. His advice is to point the rod down and jerk the lure with the rod tip, then recoil the tip and point it right back at the lure. He says that when you do this, you throw slack into the line. Kevin points out that the slack makes the lure stop, and the next jerk makes it move forward to the other side. If done quickly, the lure will dance back and forth, the slack allowing it to travel from side to side to get a wider action. Also, Kevin explains that as you jerk down on the bait, you are driving it down to its deepest diving depth. "Most people, when fishing with this technique, are constantly reeling the lure," the pro states. "You need to jerk and then reel up only the slack line. I never pull the bait toward the boat with the reel, only the rod" (Illustration 2.1).

The young pro tries to get the bass to dictate the retrieve they want on a given day. As far as the rhythm goes, he thinks the more erratic the better. VanDam uses a slightly different retrieve for varying water clarities. "If the water is clear, I like to fish the lure a little faster and make the fish come up for it," states VanDam. "In fifteen feet of water, a deep crankbait that dives ten feet will come close to the fish, and they can scrutinize the lure in the extremely clear water.

Illustration 2.1 *Kevin retrieves the jerkbait with his rod held low and by twitching or jerking the rod tip. He retrieves and moves the lure forward only with the rod, using the reel to take up the slack line.*

"On the other hand, if your jerkbait only dives three feet or so, a bass has to come up to it. Looking up at the lure against the surface of the water tends to break up the profile of the lure so that the bass doesn't get a good look at the bait." Kevin feels one of the most important things to remember when fishing the jerkbait is to choose and work your lure *above the bass*. "You can't have your lure run on the same level as the bass," adds Kevin, "and you definitely don't want your lure going deeper than the bass. You want the bass to come up for your lure. This is a natural action for a bass, since they move up to chase schools of baitfish or individual stragglers." VanDam says that on the Great Lakes he used to bring smallmouth bass up from twenty feet of water to strike a jerkbait running only three feet deep. He adds that fishing deep crankbaits, on these same fish, is not nearly as effective (Illustration 2.2).

In dingy water, VanDam uses a different approach. Since bass can't see the lure from a distance, he tries to zero in on

Illustration 2.2 *Bass can be coaxed to rise from a considerable depth to strike a jerkbait retrieved overhead.*

ambush points, such as brush, blowdowns, rocks, and other cover. He tries to fish the lure as close to the cover as possible. He tends to use a brighter colored lure and a more methodical action. When the lure approaches cover, Kevin will try to get the bait to dance back and forth as erratically as possible. When the lure is close to the cover, he tries to keep it in the strike zone as long as possible by slowing the retrieve and giving a sharp jerk to the bait. This gives the fish more time to see it and come and get it.

When a bass strikes a jerkbait, you seldom feel the strike. Kevin believes it's because most strikes occur when you have thrown the lure slack line with your rod. Kevin says, "Most of the time you will just feel a dead weight or a heavy feeling on the line. You don't have to set the hook hard. When I get a strike, I just pull into the fish. The fish almost hooks himself, and all you need to do is apply a steady pull."

JERKBAITS FOR SPRING, SUMMER, AND FALL

When asked about fishing the jerkbait throughout the season, Kevin replies, "Water temperature and water clarity are the two things that impact my jerkbait fishing more than anything. I never fish a jerkbait until the surface water temperature is above fifty degrees." Kevin adds that in the spring, in clear water, when the water is cold, you need a lure that will stay close to the bass and stay in the strike zone longer, which means fishing shallower water. He also states that you need to slow your retrieve down a bit, and you may need to use a lure that runs a little deeper if the fish are not in real shallow water.

VanDam states that when the clear water warms, in the summer and fall, again fish your lure fairly fast and keep it above the bass. "I like to parallel-cast down rocky banks as well as parallel-cast weed beds, boat docks, and rip-rapped banks," he says. "The parallel-casting method allows me to keep the bait in the strike zone longer (Illustration 2.3). Also, I can cover a lot of water with this technique. That's one of the reasons I really concentrate on it." Kevin emphasizes that when the water is real dingy, the bass have a tendency to stay shallow almost all year. He says to fish bright baits slowly around cover.

The Michigan pro loves to fish this technique in the clear waters of the northern states and feels that, pure and simple, it is the most effective and predictable method to cover more water and catch more bass. Kevin also thinks this technique is as predictable as a "southerner ordering grits for breakfast." VanDam states flatly, "Eighty percent of the days I've been on

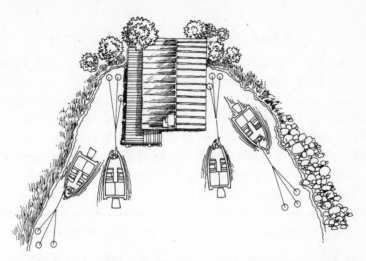

Illustration 2.3 *Parallel casts to cover such areas as grassbeds, boathouses, or rip-rapped banks keep your lure in the strike zone longer.*

these clear northern waters, I've caught bass on jerkbaits. One reason this technique is so good, although it is becoming more and more popular, is because few people stay with it and develop it to its potential." The pro points out that fishing a jerkbait all day is physically demanding and that there are a lot of intricacies in fishing the bait that make a difference. He also says a positive to fishing this bait is that bass don't seem to get real educated by the lure the way they have by other lures. An example of a lure that bass become educated about is a buzzbait, which was great bait before the bass learned to stay away from it. VanDam says that on the pro level, he sees the jerkbait technique getting stronger and stronger since it is so effective at putting bass in the boat.

JERKBAITS AND THE WEATHER

Aside from spring cold fronts and late fall snowstorms, both of which affect water temperature, and a torrential rain, which muddies the whole lake, weather doesn't hinder this technique much. VanDam points out that wind can break up the water surface so that you may need to go with a flashy bait, but you only need to be able to adjust your choice of lures for those sunny or cloudy situations. VanDam won the New York Top 100 B.A.S.S. Tournament fishing jerkbaits almost exclusively. He had to keep switching colors for sunny and cloudy conditions so that the fish could see the lure to the maximum under each set of conditions.

WHAT ABOUT WEIGHTING THE JERKBAIT?

The newest craze in the jerkbait technique is to apply weights of one sort or another in order to sink your lure and hold it at a particular depth. Kevin has been experimenting with weighting his lures for years. He feels the premise behind the weights is to get your lure to suspend in the bass strike zone rather than having the lure float up as you jerk it on the retrieve. VanDam points out that the lures on the market that are supposed to suspend right out of the box have limitations. For example, Kevin researched one of these and found it would suspend on retrieve in water that is 55 degrees. However, in water 70 degrees it floated.

He likes the new Suspend Dots, manufactured by Storm Lures. These are lead weights configured as either dots or strips. VanDam says that you can apply these dots to the lures in various spots and get different action (Illustration 2.4). Aside from helping the lure suspend, you can apply a dot behind the diving plate and the lures will nose down, giving you a different action on retrieve. In most cases, VanDam does not try to weight a lure to get a perfect suspending quality. Instead, he utilizes the weights to fine-tune a lure or give it a different action. Kevin states, "Every

Illustration 2.4 *One method to make your bait suspend is to attach lead stick-on weight(s).*

angler needs some of the stick-on weights in his tackle box. You can use them to change the action of all types of lures, not just jerkbaits." The pro also feels that the best way to modify your jerkbaits is to go to a swimming pool to test them out. This will let you see how the weights modify the action and how deep it will suspend under certain water temperatures.

DO IT YOUR WAY

Kevin's advice to anglers heading to the lake is, "Do it your way!" He explains, "You need to go out and determine your own solutions to the fishing puzzle, instead of going to the marina or tackle shop or calling your buddy to get advice on what lure to use or how deep to fish. You need to figure out what the patterns are at any given time. You need to do the work and do it on your own. Every day the conditions are different and the bass react differently. There is no shortcut, and solving your own puzzles will help make you a better bass fisherman."

Kevin loves the excitement of catching bass, but what really turns him on is to go out and determine what gets the bass to strike on a given day. He takes into account weather and water conditions, the time of year and all the different variables. Just what will it take to get the bass to open his mouth and strike on that given day? To Kevin VanDam, a two-time B.A.S.S. Angler of the Year at twenty-eight years of age, that's the ultimate thrill in bass fishing!

Jimmy Houston considers spinnerbaits his ace in the hole for
taking bass under a variety of conditions.

3

JIMMY HOUSTON

Serious Bass Fishing's Spinnerbait King

In the world of professional bass fishing, Jimmy Houston's a whole lot more than just another pretty face. Houston's media fame has never overshadowed what his fellow competitors know for a fact: Jimmy's the virtuoso of spinnerbait fishing, the man who developed many of the trends and techniques that today's serious anglers take for granted.

Without a doubt Houston has turned an unforgettable giggle and a proclivity to kiss his catch on camera into a recognizable fame that's influenced an entire generation of anglers. Yet Jimmy the serious angler remains a fisherman's fisherman, who got to the top the hard way. He's a man who's done his homework; he's a spinnerbait devotee who's developed tech-

**JIMMY
HOUSTON**
COOKSON,
OKLAHOMA

*Two-time B.A.S.S.
Angler of the Year.
Holder of thirteen
national bass-fishing
titles. Fourteen-time
BASS Masters Classic
Finalist. Host of the
television series* Jimmy
Houston Outdoors.

niques that others stand in line to copy. Most of all, Houston's a pro who still proves his expertise on the water under the toughest of competitive conditions . . . and still earns a check at the end of most tournaments.

Jimmy's fabled career as a professional fisherman has roots firmly planted in the red-dirt soil of central Oklahoma. It's almost as if angling came as naturally as breathing. In fact Houston can't even remember when he didn't fish. His was a fishing family, and the entire clan delved the depths together: mom, dad, Jimmy's uncles, and an entire armada of kids. Home away from home was the nearest creek bank, and the family baited up for just about anything that swam—catfish, bass, crappie, bream. These early expeditions were down-home, country-style fishing in the truest sense, a fact Jimmy credits with providing a solid, broad-based background for his professional career.

Today Houston may be Mr. Magic when he casts his custom baitcast rigs. But way back in his formative years young Jimmy was pushing the button on a spincast outfit. This was an eagerly awaited step up from the cane pole and can of worms that tamed those initial prairie-pool sunfish.

Those were the days when Houston started stocking up a storehouse of memories. Today he may be one of bass fishing's most recognized disciples. Yet he's never forgotten the thrill of watching a bobber disappear underwater while a breeze played in the cottonwood leaves. Nor the day his grandfather decided to demonstrate a prized possession: one of those newfangled spincast reels that were guaranteed not to backlash.

"We'd gone to my granddad's house," Houston reminisces, "and he'd bought himself one of the first Zebco reels—it had a button on the top that you pushed to release the line, and a ball that rolled around on the back to control the speed and distance. We went out behind his house, and granddad could cast that thing from the back door almost down to the outhouse. And in those days, that was a long way!" It wasn't much longer before Houston had one of those newfangled spincast concoctions of his own, the perfect tool to help fine-tune his ever-growing love of fishing.

FROM PASSION TO PROFESSION: HOUSTON HITS THE TOURNAMENT TRAIL

After graduating from high school in Oklahoma City, Jimmy headed for the greener pastures of eastern Oklahoma, where he'd make his home in Tahlequah near Lake Tenkiller. It proved to be the perfect match of personality and place, because the lake was a mecca for aspiring bass pros, and Houston was undeniably eager. Houston and his wife, Chris, set up housekeeping in those green hills, and Jimmy started selling insurance. Yet even when business flourished, Houston felt a sense of frustration. He knew he had the angling talent to become a serious pro, but there simply wasn't enough free time to compete.

In 1975 Jimmy decided to roll the dice and take enough time off to enter every professional tournament held that year. It was a gamble that paid dividends, because the young pro from Cherokee County was good enough to finish a lofty third in the overall standings.

In 1976 an even more confident and serious Jimmy Houston was once again on hand to participate in the entire tourney slate and continue his domination. At the end of the year, Houston was, without a doubt, the very best bass fisherman in the world. His amassed winnings were unequaled, and Jimmy was in the limelight. He won the much-coveted B.A.S.S. Angler of the Year award. It was a fantastic way to launch a professional career, and all those lights that illuminated Houston's growing fame just never seemed to dim.

Others of Jimmy's status have spurned the tough bass-fishing tournament trail, but not Jimmy. "The reason I love bass fishing is because it's fun. I still get a kick out of catchin 'em today," Houston says. His down-home approach is genuine, and people sense it. He just loves people. Just watch him "work" the crowd at a BASS Masters Classic launching or a weigh-in, telling jokes and interacting with everyone. Jimmy keeps his sense of humor whether he's winning or losing. After a particularly bad day at a major tournament, he quipped, "I knew I was in trouble when I backlashed the toilet paper at the motel this morning."

Today Jimmy Houston is on the verge of becoming a national treasure. Part of the fame stems from the personalized folklore that he's worked hard to promote. You'll never see Jimmy refuse an autograph or ignore any fan. However, it would be a mistake to forget about Jimmy Houston the serious fisherman. Take it from the pros who still compete against him: Houston's spinnerbait techniques remain the standard that perhaps dozens of "wannabe" young pros struggle to match.

Jimmy isn't shy about singing the praises of spinnerbait fishing. He believes in the bait's versatility and proven track record, just as he believes that most fishermen would bring more bass to the boat if they'd just get on the spinnerbait bandwagon. "I suspect that in tournaments, more bass are caught on spinnerbaits year-round than on any other lure," Houston says. Ask him why, and Jimmy's quick to give plenty of good reasons.

SPINNERBAIT VERSATILITY:
WHY THE LURE REMAINS
JIMMY'S ALL-AROUND WINNER

First of all, Houston points out, spinnerbaits don't discriminate when it comes to size. He says you'll catch both large and small fish, and there's always a good chance that at some time during the day a really big fish will hit the bait. Houston believes that the best approach is also the most simple: Just try to catch a limit, and let size take care of itself. He feels that if you follow this strategy consistently, you'll catch good numbers as well as quality-size bass.

Houston also likes the fact that fishermen can cover lots of water with a spinnerbait. It's a lure that can be fished deep as well as shallow, and it's effective on both fast and slow retrieves. He attributes much of his fishing success to these qualities. "I've been accused of being hyperactive. I don't know if that's true, but a spinnerbait fits my need to move and present the lure to the bass as many times as possible," states Houston.

Above all, Jimmy believes that spinnerbaits are extremely versatile: They'll work into whatever strategy you decide to employ. The baits provide much-needed adaptability for pro fishermen, who face varying lake conditions all over the continent, in all kinds of weather, and at all times of the year. In fact, Jimmy believes that no other lure produces fish under a greater variety of weather conditions, water clarity, water depths, and types of cover than does a spinnerbait. It could be the most versatile lure known to man.

A lot of pros like to make some sort of natural connection between artificial baits and natural forage in the bass food chain. But Houston shrugs off any comparison between spinnerbaits and biological factors. He doesn't think the lure imitates anything natural . . . and believes that maybe that's the key to the smashing strikes they produce. "I don't spend much time trying to match blade sizes to forage fish," Houston claims. "I know some pros do, but in most spinnerbait situations [stained-to-murky water] I don't. To me, vibration and flash are the key.

"I think the bait may be a little bit intimidating to bass, which could be why they strike at them so viciously, particularly in shallow water," Houston says. "There's no way of knowing for sure, but maybe the fish just don't like having the baits around." Jimmy also has some strong opinions when it comes to color. He likes combinations of chartreuse or white, or even the two colors together. His favorite combo remains chartreuse matched with blue. After that, Houston often turns to some sort of perch shade.

SHORT-, REGULAR-, AND LONG-ARM SPINNERBAITS

A long-arm spinnerbait has a wire to which the blade is attached, extending all the way back past the point of the hook. This long-arm feature enables the lure to crawl through brush and cover with a minimum of hang-ups.

The regular-arm spinnerbait has a blade wire that extends just short of the point of the hook. It, too, is very snag-resistant and is the design used by most pros. Since most of Houston's spinnerbait fishing is done in shallow, brushy water, he usually prefers these regular-arm models.

The short-arm baits have a limited application, but can be ideal for falling or helicoptering (see section on spinnerbait retrieves). The blade wire on these lures extends back only about halfway to the point of the hook (Illustration 3.1).

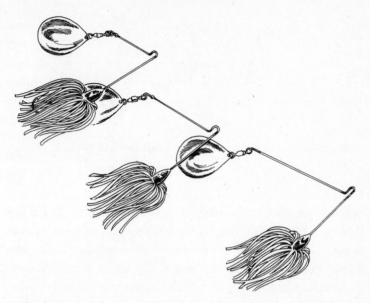

Illustration 3.1 *For different purposes, spinnerbaits have varying lengths of the wire arm to which the spinner is attached. Shown here are the short-arm, the regular-arm, and the long-arm spinnerbaits.*

CHOOSING A BLADE: JIMMY OUTLINES SEVERAL BIG BASS COMBINATIONS

The Tahlequah-based pro uses all types of blades, but he prefers any from among a variety of round styles over the willowleaf spinners. "I probably use a Tennessee blade or a Colorado blade a little bit more than the others," Houston says. "But all styles certainly have their uses."

For instance, Jimmy says that willowleaf spinners move through grass more efficiently, while round blades seem to produce more vibration. With this in mind, Houston says you need

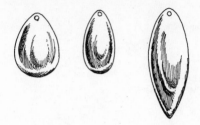

Illustration 3.2 *Different blade shapes create flash and vibration. Shown* (left to right) *are the Colorado, Indiana, and willowleaf blades.*

to key in on what you're attempting to accomplish with the bait. Willowleaf blades produce more flash and reveal more surface. Round blades give better vibrations when visibility is dim. And if you need a lot more visual stimulus, such as in muddy water, go to colored blades in chartreuse or fluorescent reds and oranges. Blades are the spinnerbait component that I see changing in future years. Already we are seeing wedge blades and hinged blades, but I expect we will see blades made from new metals and materials that will increase flash and vibration (Illustration 3.2).

Personally, Houston prefers spinnerbaits that produce vibration. When the spinnerbait blade spins and rotates, it causes the wire shaft holding the swivel and blade to wiggle and move. These two elements send out sound-wave vibration through the water, which can be picked up and felt by a bass.

Houston likes to have a touch of red in all his baits, because he feels the color triggers strikes. He's not overly opinionated when it comes to spinnerbait size, and remains content to use whatever fits the conditions he's fishing. However, if the TV personality does have a favorite, it's a quarter-ounce lure. "If you're casting into a stiff wind, then you may need a heavier bait," Houston points out. "But if I'm fishing in conditions that allow short, accurate casts, then I prefer the quarter-ounce size."

Illustration 3.3 *Houston knows a trailer hook can help catch those "short" strikes. Here, a piece of surgical rubber is cut and placed over the eye of the trailer hook. The point of the spinnerbait hook is then forced through the rubber and the eye of the trailer hook.*

THE IMPORTANCE OF TRAILER HOOKS

Jimmy uses a trailer hook 100 percent of the time when he is fishing spinnerbaits. "I use a hook slightly smaller than the spinnerbait hook. I force a piece of surgical tubing over the eye of the trailer hook and then insert my spinnerbait hook," states Houston. Jimmy is also quick to point out that a trailer hook catches short strikes, but it also has a down side. He says that it gives the bait a little different feel, probably because of wind resistance, and this can make it more difficult to cast if you're not used to it. If you use it all the time, you will learn to cast with it being there. The average angler usually fishes a spinnerbait without the trailer hook and then they put it on when they think they need it. This can play havoc with casting accuracy (Illustration 3.3).

TACKLE, LINE, AND TECHNIQUE

Jimmy also prefers 5½-foot pistol-grip rods and will sometimes go up to a six-footer. He's generally tied on with fourteen-pound test Trilene XT. "Sometimes, in clear-water lakes, I might drop down to twelve-pound test," Houston says. "And during those times of the year when you can catch really big bass in heavy cover, I'll go up to seventeen- and even twenty-pound test line."

The famed pro fisherman looks upon his favorite lure principally as a shallow-water bait. "I generally don't fish my spinnerbaits deep. When I do need to go deep, I do it with other lures. However, at times, I will slow-roll one of these baits deep," Houston says.

Often the Oklahoma angler seeks out heavy cover that presents difficult casting situations. He says he likes to catch fish that other fishermen have missed, or have failed to work properly. "At the professional level, overall skills are too good to follow behind other fishermen and pick up fish," Jimmy says. "Yet at the general level, if you learn to excel at casting, you'll be able to catch fish that others have left. The ability to cast to an exact spot and work your lure very close to a submerged log, stump, or rock may draw a strike. Less-skilled caster's lures will not entice a fish holding tight on cover."

HOUSTON'S FISHING INNOVATIONS

There are two bass-fishing innovations that can be traced directly to Jimmy Houston. The first is the "no front seat" approach to bass fishing. In the 1970s, Jimmy appeared somewhat strange for not even carrying any kind of a seat for the front deck of his bass boat. Instead he preferred to stand up all day and fish. He felt it gave him an advantage in seeing cover, making casts, and hooking and controlling a bass. Today, almost every pro angler agrees with that concept. And while some use the extended pole and "butt seats," most have emulated Jimmy's stand-up approach.

The other innovation Jimmy brought to bass fishing is his famous underhanded cast. Just watch one episode of Jimmy's

ESPN TV show, *Jimmy Houston Outdoors,* and you will see the advantages of this cast come to life. Instead of lifting his rod and casting the lure, either directly overhead or three-quarter arm, as most anglers do, Jimmy lowers his rod as the lure retrieve is ending. He then lifts the lure only a few inches off the water, spins his wrist to the right (he is a right-handed caster), and moves his arm slightly forward as the lure completes its rotation on the end of the line. At the same time he releases the free-spool thumb bar on his free-spool reel. The result is a cast that shoots out only inches above the water. Jimmy "feathers" his cast in by applying slight pressure to the turning reel spool with his thumb. The result is more casts per hour, with more accuracy and an always splashless entry. It takes practice, but it can be achieved. The underhanded cast is now a standard among professional bass fishermen.

WIND, WEATHER, WATER: JIMMY TALKS ABOUT READING THE CONDITIONS . . .

Like all accomplished anglers, Houston keeps an eye on the weather. He points out that changing conditions can have a dramatic effect on how you fish spinnerbaits, due to how fronts cause fish to relate to cover. Good spinnerbait fishermen know that bright, sunny "bluebird" days following a front usually find fish holding tight on cover. In this situation your spinnerbait needs to penetrate the cover, bump the brush, and in general be retrieved as tight to the cover as possible. Cloudy, windy days seem to loosen their grip somewhat and result in an expanded strike zone, allowing for a little less finesse and usually a little more productivity.

. . . AND CHOOSING A SPINNERBAIT ARSENAL TO MATCH

Houston believes that a basic spinnerbait arsenal should begin with a ¼-ounce bait with a single gold blade and a chartreuse and blue skirt. Next he includes a ⅜-ounce bait, with a gold or copper blade and some nickel on the shaft, in a combination of chartreuse and white. Finally he makes sure his tackle box contains a ¾-ounce spinnerbait with a chartreuse or white head and a combination chartreuse and white skirt. "I'll vary the size of blades on these three lures, so I can switch them around and make a lot of different baits," Houston is quick to add. "Beginning fishermen forget that you can change blades around. For example, you can take a quarter-ounce spinnerbait and put a really big blade on it and you'll end up with a totally different type of bait. Or you can take a half-ounce or five-eighths-ounce bait and put a small blade on it and trim down the skirt, and you'll have a small, heavy lure that will really cut through the wind on bad days."

HOUSTON SHARES A TRICK OR TWO

Over the years Houston has picked up a few tricks that make his spinnerbait fishing more productive, including opening the hook up just a touch for a better bite when fish strike. He also likes to increase the angle in the bend of the wire for more vibration, and he flattens out the ends of his round blades to achieve the same effect. "Don't fall into the trap of using the bait just like it comes from the store," Jimmy urges. "Do some trial-and-error experimenting to find out what really works. You may want to add a plastic trailer. You can experiment with different-size and -shape blades." Houston's casting style and skill are legendary. Still, he'll be the first to tell you that it's

Illustration 3.4 *The "slow-rolling" retrieve is accomplished by allowing the lure to sink and then retrieving it slowly and allowing it to crawl over underwater cover.*

equally important to entice a strike through a variety of retrieves.

SPINNERBAIT RETRIEVES

SLOW-ROLLING (ILLUSTRATION 3.4)

Water clarity determines the depth of retrieve. Houston occasionally lets his spinnerbaits run really slow and deep, sometimes as much as fifteen feet, particularly when fishing concrete structures like bridge pilings. The Tahlequah pro sometimes resorts to a slow roll in the spring months, when he feels that bigger fish are hanging out in water that's four to seven feet deep. Slow-rolling a spinnerbait requires that you allow the lure to sink to the bottom and climb over cover such as rocks, logs, or brush. When he's slow-rolling, Jimmy turns to a bigger spinnerbait, such as a ¾-ounce lure or maybe even up to 1 full ounce. He uses a large trailer behind the bait. He makes his cast, then slowly reels the lure back, following the contour of the bottom, or maybe speeding up a little to bring the bait over the top of some submerged cover.

Illustration 3.5 *"Falling" a spinnerbait can be used in combination with other retrieves. The idea is to kill the retrieve of the lure and allow it to fall past a stump, rock, or other potential fish-holding cover.*

FALLING OR DROPPING (ILLUSTRATION 3.5)

This retrieve can be used anytime you encounter cover with your lure. Sometimes you can actually see the log or stump you want your lure to "fall" over. As your lure moves along and crosses a piece of cover, kill the retrieve and let the lure fall just past the object. The spinner will spin and the skirt will flare, emulating an injured prey. At times bass can't resist.

HELICOPTERING (ILLUSTRATION 3.6)

This is similar to falling, but it is done with a short-arm spinnerbait. Again, run your lure past the cover, and again allow the lure to fall. The shorter arm on the spinnerbait gives the

Illustration 3.6 *The "helicoptering" retrieve is usually accomplished with the short arm spinnerbait. The lure is allowed to fall to the bottom with the blade helicoptering down. The spinnerbait is then lifted quickly off the bottom and allowed to helicopter down again. The process is continued throughout the retrieve. Most strikes come as the lure helicopters down.*

blade a different angle and you get a "helicoptering" effect. This is very effective at the edge of a drop-off. Also, this can be used in areas with little cover. You can jerk the bait up from the bottom and let it helicopter back, continuing the process throughout the retrieve.

BULGING OR WAKING (ILLUSTRATION 3.7)

At times this is dynamite! Here you retrieve the lure just below the surface to the point that the spinning blade "bulges" water

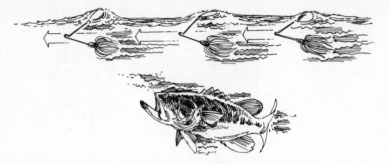

Illustration 3.7 A *spinnerbait retrieved quickly just under the surface creates a bulge or wake. This can be a dynamite retrieve when used over a grass- or weedbed.*

above the surface. The blade does not break the surface, but creates a bulge and a wake. Bass will rise and strike this retrieve with a bull rush!

LINE OF SIGHT (ILLUSTRATION 3.8)

This retrieve is Jimmy's favorite. Here you keep the lure in sight and bring it as close to cover and ambush points as possible. The retrieve speed can be fast, medium, or slow. Try them all. Jimmy will actually make the lure bump the bush or log. When your lure strikes cover and glances off to the side, hold on tight. This is an excellent way to trigger a strike.

DETECTING A STRIKE

Ask Houston how he detects a strike and he'll give you a typically straight Houston answer: "When they jerk the rod right out of my hands!" Press him and he'll become a bit more technical. "First of all, I generally have the bait in sight so that I can see the fish hit it," Houston explains. "You need to remember not to jerk the bait too soon when you see a fish strike: that's a common error." Jimmy adds that, in clear-water con-

Illustration 3.8 *Perhaps Jimmy's favorite is the simple "line of sight" retrieve. He keeps the lure in sight at all times and tries to make contact with fish holding cover. Most of the time you will actually see the fish strike.*

ditions, bass often come up behind a bait and just grab on and hold it. His advice is to wait until the fish turns its head either left or right before setting the hook. Otherwise you'll miss a lot of good opportunities.

JIMMY ON THE MIND GAME

Houston's big on technique, but he's quick to point out that every angler is born with something much more important in his or her fishing arsenal: tenacity. This is the key, he says: Just don't ever give up. There will be good days and bad days, and you'll learn from both. "Be willing to experiment and adapt to changing patterns and conditions," he says. "Do that, and you'll soon be on the road to becoming a serious and accomplished bass angler. The biggest mistake anglers make is to lose their positive mental outlook," says Houston. "I think this accounts for a lot of my success. No matter how long I've fished, I always think the next cast will produce the big bass."

When it comes to fishing, Jimmy knows serious. Just ask

his wife. After all, we're talking about a man who once held a finger over a bleeding cut on his spouse's forehead just so that she could keep on boating big fish.

Of course Jimmy will admit that, at times, there's been a little luck involved. Like the day in Texas when his cameraman begged to borrow a hot lure that was catching all kinds of big bass and Jimmy told him no, partly out of mischief and partly because he was down to his last pattern of that particular blade. However, the cameraman continued to entreat, so Houston relented with a word of caution: "Lose this bait and you're dead." On the cameraman's first cast, a six-pound bass smashed the lure and promptly broke off, and Houston gave his assistant a stony, "I told you so" stare. The photographer urged his boss to throw back to the spot where the water was still swirling and catch the fish again, but Jimmy was still considering how hard it would be to shove his helper out of the boat.

A few minutes later, and mostly out of reflex, Houston did manage to flip a jig in the vicinity of where the six-pounder disappeared. He was greeted with a strike that jarred both elbows. When the bass was in the boat, both men could clearly see that the jig was lodged in one side of the jaw and the prized spinnerbait was still dangling from the other. That's the kind of excitement that Jimmy Houston brings to organized fishing . . . and why cameramen like to work for him.

Houston's not afraid to talk about the foibles of fishing, because he's the first to admit that it's a game you really can't conquer. Jimmy feels that "bass are becoming more educated. You know, they say that there are two kinds of bass in every lake, the catchable and the uncatchable. I don't believe any bass is uncatchable, but I can see that the larger bass are beginning to shy away from certain lures they see a lot. Here is where customizing your lures really comes into play. Give the bait a slightly different look, action, or vibration and it can make a difference." Techniques have to be addressed and formulated again and again, and Jimmy thinks even the fish are beginning to display a lot more individuality—just like their favorite TV fisherman, if you're willing to believe a man who'll kiss a bass.

Larry Nixon, bass fishing's all-time money winner, relies on
plastic worms to help him find and catch bass.

4

LARRY NIXON

Wizard with a Plastic Worm

Those who have fished with him, against him, or written of his angling exploits all tend to agree: The Wizard of Bee Branch, also known as Larry Nixon, can cast a spell with bass tackle that leaves the competition bobbing in his wake. Bee Branch is a small town in north-central Arkansas, just down the road from Greer's Ferry Reservoir, now better known as the launching pad for Nixon's fabled fishing career.

Larry has consistently cornered the pot of gold on the pro Bass Anglers Sportsman Society (B.A.S.S.) tournament circuit, capturing a BASS Masters Classic crown, garnering B.A.S.S. Angler of the Year, earning the title of Best Overall Angler on the B.A.S.S. circuit, and repeatedly

LARRY NIXON
BEE BRANCH,
ARKANSAS

Bass fishing's all-time leading money winner. Two-time B.A.S.S. Angler of the Year, BASS Masters Classic, and four-time Megabucks Champion. Fourteen-time BASS Masters Classic Finalist. Seventy-three percent of professional anglers voted Nixon America's best bass fisherman.

sweeping the Megabucks competitions. Today he continues to be rated as one of the top plastic-worm fishermen in the world.

Year in and year out, Nixon turns to his finely tuned worm techniques to remain a top money winner in what can often be a frustrating way to make a living. Yet for Nixon, fishing the pro B.A.S.S. circuit remains a labor of love, one that still provides emotional rewards as well as the tangible prizes he takes to the bank. And it's all due to wizardry, like the way he can make a plastic worm do his bidding. For legions of bass large and small, Nixon's tempting presentations are just too much to bear. So they bite. And the Wizard of Bee Branch wins big. Big enough to become an American fishing legend!

THE BEGINNINGS OF AN ARKANSAS LEGEND

Even legends have to start somewhere, and for Nixon it all began in the green hills of Arkansas, a state blessed with fabled fishing waters. Fortunately for Larry, some of the best were always close at hand.

Nixon remembers starting his angling education at the same time he started deciphering his ABCs. Larry was six years old when he began taking fishing seriously. With lots of encouragement from his father, also an avid angler, the young Arkansan from Bee Branch began to develop his fishing instincts. Larry waded creeks that fed the nearby Red River and haunted every local stock pond that held bass. Any waters within walking distance were his classroom. He'd trudge overland, a spinning outfit over his shoulder, a tackle box loaded with baits, such as Water Hags, Abu Spinners, and Lucky 13s, in his hand.

Day after day, year after year, this is how Larry Nixon did his down-home, Arkansas-style homework. He'll tell you today that he probably learned as much from those early days of fishing as anything he's experienced since. It's a pattern that most of the world's best anglers always seem to fall into, one that starts with a sheer love of fishing, then builds into a fierce desire to be the best.

CATCHING PRO FEVER

When he was sixteen years old, Nixon took the next big step toward a career as a professional bass angler. He and a couple of friends began to haunt nearby Greer's Ferry Reservoir, borrowing their fathers' boats and spending entire weekends on the water.

Catching bass in big, man-made reservoirs required an entirely new set of angling skills, and Nixon and his friends learned through sheer, dogged determination. The new reservoir required knowledge of bass movements and how they related to the thousands of acres of flooded timber, creek channels, and exposed flats. By the time he was in his early twenties, Nixon, now a college student, had earned enough of a reputation to be in demand as a weekend fishing guide.

Things were happening fast in the world of bass fishing while Larry Nixon struggled to decide which way to direct his professional life. Larry was finding it difficult to choose a college major, especially after his bassin' buddies moved farther south, down to the newly filled and bass-laden East Texas lakes Sam Rayburn and Toledo Bend.

So, early in the 1970s, Nixon decided to arrange for a Christmas vacation with his old pals and try out some of the red-hot Lone Star fishing he'd heard so much about. As a result of that trip, Nixon spent about six days testing his skills against Toledo Bend bass, a week that changed his life forever. "That was the most awesome fishing I've seen in my whole life," Nixon recalls. "As a result, I wasn't worth a hoot in school the next semester. All I could think about was going back to Toledo Bend and becoming a guide there."

In 1972 Nixon returned to the East Texas lake of his dreams, planning to spend a couple of months working as a guide and hoping the change of scenery might clear up some of his indecision regarding college.

A FEW BUMPS IN A FABLED CAREER

However, it proved to be a one-way trip. Nixon never returned to the campus; the fishing was just too good and guides were in such demand that the young Arkansan decided that the bass in Toledo Bend had made his career decisions for him.

Following several years of guiding, Nixon decided to test the water and turn pro. There were stone-broke days when he questioned his decision, and nights when he wondered where he'd sleep. Still, Larry stuck it out on the B.A.S.S. tournament trail and began to convert time-proven techniques into cash money. Most of those dollars were earned through the benefit of a few inches of bright plastic. Nixon used a plastic worm to eventually wrangle enough bass to win the B.A.S.S. Angler of the Year title, not to mention four Megabucks Championships and even a BASS Masters Classic victory. Today he ranks as professional bass fishing's all-time leading money winner, having won well over $1.2 million fishing for the elusive bass. Because of his success, his advice on worm tackle, baits, and presentation is as eagerly sought as another Elvis sighting in the South.

Despite Nixon's great success in professional bass fishing, he still just loves to fish. "I think one of the reasons bass fishing is so important to me is that it allows me to be in control of my choices," says Nixon. "Being outside and around Mother Nature doesn't hurt either."

NIXON ON WHY WORMS
ARE AN ALL-AROUND WINNER

Nixon believes that if an angler commits himself to the plastic-worm technique, he will ultimately catch more fish. "I think it's the most versatile technique, and it's the type of presentation that is required the largest percentage of the time throughout the year," states Nixon. "It will catch a few fish when they're not biting and it's even better when they are biting. It's a technique that will produce fish almost all year-round, with the possible exception of winter. This is not to say that the other techniques are not good and important, but if you become real proficient with a plastic worm, you won't regret it."

Nixon believes that bass can be taken on worms in any situation where the fish are bunched together in a particular area. Some of the best bets, he says, are grass beds, submerged contour lines that form points, underwater brushpiles, bridge pilings, or any other fish-attracting structure that might hold more than one bass. "Those are situations where I'm definitely going to use a plastic worm," Nixon says. "I feel a worm is my mandatory 'go to' bait anytime I'm presenting a lure to schooling bass."

Nixon also turns to his plastic-worm arsenal when fish are holding on wood or some other heavy cover. "Fish holding on wood will hit a worm even when they won't come up and hit a topwater lure or chase a spinnerbait," Nixon points out. "When bass won't hit other lures, then plastic worms become essential. They'll get you those hard-to-catch fish, and they'll also catch greater numbers."

RIGGING UP:
A FEW NIXON POINTERS ON COLOR

Larry fishes the majority of his worms Texas-rigged, or with the hook buried in the bait so that it stays virtually snagproof. Above the worm he rigs a bullet weight that slides freely on the line.

Nixon feels that water color should determine the color of the bait. "In dingy or dark water, I prefer worms with colored tails—fluorescent tails, such as chartreuse, fire tails, and blue tails—and a lot of glitter. In clear water I rarely resort to multitones. I use a single color with glitter in it or electric blue," he points out. Larry is quick to add that as a general rule of thumb, the darker the water, the darker the worm. In clear water he prefers lighter shades.

Throughout his many successful bass-fishing years, Nixon's best bait has remained that old standby, the purple worm. "I'll use it in shades that vary from a light purple to a really dark grape color," he says. "Purple, along with black and blue, will produce fish just about anywhere across the country."

Larry chooses the size of his worm according to the reputation of the water he's about to fish. If the lake has lots of twelve- to thirteen-inch fish, Nixon starts out with a four- to a six-inch worm. If the lake is known for really big fish, then he'll rig an eight-inch worm, sometimes opting for a nine- or even a ten-inch offering.

WORM FASHION FOR BIG FISH:
STYLE *AND* SUBSTANCE

The wizard from Bee Branch depends on three worm styles to meet most of his bassin' needs: a straight tail, a ribbon tail, and the sickle-, or action-tail design (Illustration 4.1).

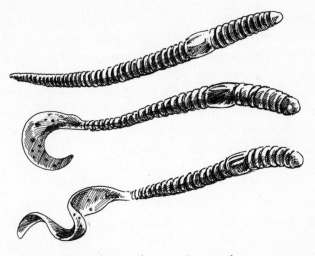

Illustration 4.1 *Depending on the time of year and water temperature, Larry Nixon utilizes three types of plastic worms* (from top to bottom): *the straight tail, the sickle tail, and the ribbon tail plastic worm.*

He says that in cold, clear water, the straight-tail worm sinks faster with less action and usually produces more strikes. As the water warms to 65 degrees or above, Nixon switches to the ribbon-tail version.

"I like the ribbon tail in grass, because it doesn't stick to the cover and has a tight swimming motion that fish seem to prefer in warmer water," Nixon says. The ribbon tail is also his choice as a worm to flip or pitch, since it rarely wraps around the cover and provides a lot of motion.

Larry reserves the sickle-tail styles for deep water, hot summer days, night fishing, dingy water, or when fishing close to cover. "I'll use this style of bait when I need something that will stir around and move a little more water," Nixon says. He adds, "Oftentimes, in these situations, the action of the worm alone is enough to entice a bass to bite."

Sometimes, primarily from February through May, Nixon may substitute a craw worm for his plastic worms. "During this time of the year you're covering two avenues with a craw worm," Nixon says. "In one way you're simulating a predator that eats the eggs in bass nests. So the fish tend to attack the bait and attempt to move it away. On the other hand, you're also simulating crawfish, a preferred bass food in the spring. It's like eating steak to folks like you and me."

HOOKS, WEIGHTS, AND OTHER HARDWARE

As for worm weights, Larry likes to make his choice according to the type of cover he intends to fish. "I base my weight choice on factors like the thickness of the cover and how deep I need to go to penetrate it," Nixon points out. "If it's thick, I'll use a heavier weight. But if the fish are sluggish or the water is dirty, dark, or really hot or cold, then fish have a tendency to suspend, and I'll use lighter weights. I also use the lighter ones when I'm after extremely shallow bass."

Nixon's standard weights include ³⁄₁₆- and ¼-ounce styles. Anything smaller stays in the tackle box until a special situation comes up. Most of the time the Bee Branch pro says he prefers to stick with the heavier weights.

WORM-FISHING TACKLE

Nixon's tackle is dictated by common sense. He prefers a six-foot-long, medium-heavy casting rod that's got plenty of what worm fishermen refer to as backbone. "The rod has to have enough backbone to get the job done—that's the key to worm fishing," Larry likes to stress. "You need sensitivity in the tip, but about three feet up the rod, it needs to take on the strength of a broomstick. If it doesn't, you'll end up missing or losing a lot of fish over the course of a year, because you couldn't feel them or you couldn't get your hook in the fish once you did."

Nixon uses 14- to 17-pound-test monofilament, green if he can see the line well, clear if he can't. In exceptionally clear lakes, Larry turns to 10-pound-test line almost exclusively.

His favorite reel is a baitcaster with a high-speed gear ratio, something in the 5:1 or 6:1 range. "I like the high-speed reels because there are times when the fish bumps the worm and runs with it toward the boat, like when a fish is guarding a bed in shallow water," Nixon says. "Or, sometimes you find yourself in a school of fish and one bumps it and takes off running, maybe because two or three of his buddies are trying to take that worm away from him. In these situations, it's hard to set the hook when you don't have a high-speed reel."

Even pros like Larry have equipment trouble with rods and reels from time to time. "Back when I was guiding, free-spool reels and bass rods were hard to come by. An outfit cost a whole day's guiding fee, so I was careful with the two I had," recalls Nixon. "I was guiding one day when a big school of fish broke water right behind the boat, chasing shad like crazy. I had a topwater plug on one rod and a jigging spoon on the other, since this was just what I had planned for. I cast the topwater bait out over the back of the boat and never got a bump. Then it occurred to me that these must be white bass. I yelled for my client to grab a spoon and threw the rod with the topwater bait on it to the floor. My topwater lure was still floating calmly about twenty feet from the boat. As I reached for my outfit that had a spoon tied on it, and prepared to cast, a large white bass slammed into my floating topwater lure. The fish hooked himself and began to drag my rod and reel over the rear of the boat. I remember stepping in my tackle box. Lures of all types went left and right as I made a mad dash to catch up with my rod before it exited over the rear of the boat. I made a long lunge and captured it just inches before it would have been gone for

good. With assorted lures hanging here and there on my cloth-
ing, I proudly turned to my client and exclaimed, 'Got it!' This
individual, who had been watching this whole thing in stunned
silence, finally said, 'I don't know how to tell you this, but when

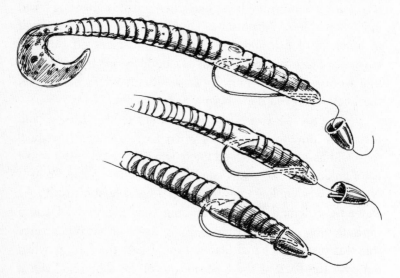

Illustration 4.2 *The Texas-rigged worm creates a lure that can actually
penetrate ambush points without hanging up. Larry does not normally peg
his worm weight but allows it to slide freely on the line. When the weight
is pegged with a toothpick, it causes the weight to remain fixed against
the head of the worm.*

you made that final lunge, you kicked your other rod and reel over the side, and it sank in seventy feet of water.'"

TO PEG OR NOT TO PEG

Nixon's not a big fan of using a toothpick to "peg" his weight in place on the line. "I just don't like to peg a weight," he says. "I'll do it in heavy cover if I want the worm to have an erratic drop. But when I'm casting, I never peg it in place." Larry says that pegged weights push up the percentage of lost fish, even though it may make casting easier. "When you set the hook with a pegged weight, all you're doing is pulling lead against the mouth and you're not getting the hook in the fish," Nixon stresses. "When the weight's not pegged, the bass will nearly always suck the worm away from the weight, and you'll hook it every time" (Illustration 4.2).

WORM FISHING TAKES SAVVY

Larry Nixon's worm-fishing technique is the envy of his peers. Yet according to the Wizard of Bee Branch, all it takes is common sense and a lot of practice. "My technique varies, depending on whether I'm target fishing, grass fishing, or structure fishing," Nixon says.

He relates that target fishing is mainly a cast into good bass cover. "I immediately drop the rod to feed the bait some slack line," Larry explains. "This allows the lure to free-fall straight down, in a natural manner, and you're going to catch more bass that way." Nixon likes to drop his rod, feed line, and watch the slack as it travels across the water, ready to detect a strike or the moment the bait reaches the bottom (Illustration 4.3). "As soon as it hits bottom, I flick my reel in gear and raise the rod tip to make sure a fish hasn't taken the worm," Larry says. "If

Illustration 4.3 *When target fishing, Larry casts to a bush or stick-up and then strips line from the reel by hand, allowing the worm to fall straight down into cover.*

nothing is there, I pick the bait up and let it fall right back down. I like to jig for three or four lifts, rarely more than a foot. Then if the cover offers the opportunity, I'll swim the worm through the limbs or logs and then drop it into another dark spot."

In the grass method, the presentation remains the same: Lower the rod, feed line, and let the bait free-fall. Nixon says that when he's swimming a worm through grass, he usually lifts the rod a bit and moves the bait over the clumps, allowing for more presentation. "I'm not attempting to finesse the fish. I'm trying to present the bait to every fish as though the bass can't see the lure coming," Larry says. "I'll swim the worm a short distance, then let it fall back down to the bottom."

When Nixon fishes structure, the presentation remains the same, except that the cast is rarely very long. "Mainly you're attempting to cover a depth that's already been established," Larry explains. "The cast is generally around thirty or forty feet, with the bait free-falling. When you're fishing a spot like a point or brush pile, you cast past it and then finesse the bait back. I try to keep the rod up a bit higher and present the worm with a short lift and some soft shaking to clear the bottom. Then I let the bait fall back down again."

Nixon stresses that he rarely raises a worm more than one or two feet while shaking it continuously. He also tries to move the lure all the way down to the breakover point where the bottom changes. "The mistake made by many anglers is to move the lure four feet or more. "Many don't realize how little move-ment is required to move a plastic worm a long way," states Nixon. "Practice in shallow water where you can see the lure. You will soon get the feel of how much effort is required to move your worm the designated distance."

"The shake can be critical," Larry says. "It's a soft twitch with the line just barely slack, just to the point where you know you're making the worm move." Nixon believes that a few hours spent casting into a swimming pool is one of the best ways to refine this technique.

Nixon doesn't mince words when it comes to hooksets: "As soon as I know it's a fish, I'm going to bust him. I don't always wait for a tug or a tap," the pro points out. "When I'm working a worm back to the boat and something produces a series of thumps, I'll ease up to find out what's there. Then if I feel pressure, I set the hook hard."

As for the hooks themselves, Nixon cautions anglers to think small. "Most beginners start with hooks that are too large, and that makes it difficult to hook fish. Try to match the hook to the size of the bait you're using, and stay with a straight-shanked worm hook if you're rigged Texas-style."

PRACTICE, PRACTICE, PRACTICE!

No doubt there's a lot that bass fishermen can learn from Larry Nixon. On the other hand, the Wizard from Bee Branch believes in a much better teacher.

"I guess my success is due to all those days spent on the water," Nixon says. "The time I spent guiding was an important part of it, because I needed the money and we went out no matter what the conditions were. But I knew I could catch fish and it didn't matter if the wind was blowing hard or if it looked like it was going to rain," the bass pro remembers. "I would still go fishing."

Larry Nixon spent three hundred days out of every year for five years on the water, no matter what the conditions, and this was before he ever competed in a professional tournament. "That's how I learned what fish do, how and when they do it, and whether there is one or maybe twenty down there," Nixon says. "You can't place a dollar figure on that kind of practical education, on those days spent on the water. They were the most important days of all for me." Larry's closing piece of advice for anglers who want to improve is to spend as much time as you can on the water. There's absolutely no substitute for hands on experience. He feels those countless hours spent on the water are the key to his success.

Denny Brauer credits the flipping and pitching techniques
for much of his success as a professional angler.

5

DENNY BRAUER

The Man Who Elevated Flipping and Pitching to an Art Form

I f you think flipping and pitching bears some relation to gymnastics or horseshoes, then you need to spend a little time with a tutor named Denny Brauer. Denny's the undisputed king of these two specialized and extremely productive bass angling techniques. They have enabled him to earn a B.A.S.S. Angler of the Year title and remain a regular at the BASS Masters Classic, that championship bass-fishing clash of skills where only the best in the world compete.

To set the record straight, flipping and pitching is simply a way of getting a specialized bait into heavy cover, like dense standing timber or flooded brush, and big bass back out of it. Both techniques present particularly good

**DENNY
BRAUER**
CAMDENTON,
MISSOURI

*1987 B.A.S.S. Angler
of the Year. 1992
BASS Masters Classic
Runner-up. Holder of
seven national bass
fishing titles. Fifteen-
time BASS Masters
Classic Finalist. 1993
Megabucks Champion.
1993 SuperStars
Champion.*

methods of coaxing inactive fish, or bass pressured by lots of angling activity, into a strike. When bass are inactive or pressured, they tend to bury down in brush and other cover. To be successful, the angler must present his lure in such a manner that it actually penetrates the bass-holding cover. Under these circumstances, a bass won't move very far to take a bait. You must literally drop it in front of his nose. The delivery often depends on finesse, and the struggle to the boat requires sheer muscle. Brauer has turned both into an art form.

A SUCCESS STORY THAT STARTED HIGH AND DRY

Brauer is a native of Nebraska, not a part of the country that is especially well known for great bass lakes. But the king of flipping and pitching never let the prairie's arid aspects keep him from his dream of competing against the best. Denny takes the view that any water big enough to hold a few catchable sport fish provides plenty of opportunity to whet a young man's appetite. Like so many of his fellow pros, Brauer caught the fever young, when he was five or six years old. Denny lived at the edge of a town near a small stream that flowed just a few hundred yards from his house. Every day, when it was warm enough, neighborhood kids would congregate along the creek and fish for whatever they could tempt to bite.

As he grew older, Brauer did his homework by reading the fishing articles flowing out of the hook 'n' bullet press. Then he'd practice what the writers preached at a series of small watershed lakes that held good numbers of hefty bass.

THE SALT BELLY STARTING GATE: BRAUER'S FIRST TASTE OF PRO COMPETITION

They called the impoundments the Salt Belly Watershed Lakes, and the flood-control structures ranged in size from two hundred acres up to twelve hundred. It was here on the Salt Bellys that Brauer got his first taste of organized competition. Denny was instrumental in starting a bass club in his home state, and then went on to win several of the group's top tournaments. Winning those events was the carrot on the stick that prodded Brauer into competing in a national tournament on Lake of the Ozarks in Missouri. The young Nebraskan, then in his midtwenties, managed a twentieth-place finish against some really tough competition. That's when he knew he could never go back to Nebraska without at least giving his dream a real chance.

Brauer moved to Lake of the Ozarks and devoted his life to the sport of bass fishing. The strong finish in his first big tournament gave him the confidence boost he needed, and Denny knew he had the skills, the drive, and the savvy to take his fishing career to the highest level. And that's where Denny Brauer, the top flipping-and-pitching expert to the rest of the pro bass crowd, has resided ever since. And why does he love bass fishing so much? "I think it is the unknown," states Brauer. "So many things you do you know exactly what the end result will be. In bass fishing nobody knows. You go out there one day and think you have it mastered and the next day you feel like you don't know anything. I think that is the intriguing part. You don't know when the next bite will be or if there is going to be one, or if you're going to go out and have the best day you've ever had. We don't know all the answers and we're constantly trying to figure out the puzzle. It's probably the most challenging sport there is when you take it to that level."

SHORT, QUIET, AND ACCURATE: BRAUER'S TECHNIQUES ARE ON TARGET FOR TOUGH BASS

Denny's chosen specialty is as hard to describe as it is incredibly effective for catching big fish. In flipping, the angler presents a lure very quietly and accurately over short distances. The length of line that is actually cast remains fixed; you control the line and presentation with your hand and rod tip rather than the reel, which remains engaged instead of free-spooling. If you're flipping fifteen feet of line, then you move the boat to within fifteen feet of the cover you intend to fish. That part is predetermined. The part that is not predetermined is the bait you choose to present, and the tangle of bass cover where you choose to present it (Illustration 5.1).

Pitching is more of a conventional cast, with the reel's spool disengaged as if you were making a traditional presentation. The difference is that pitching is also designed especially for short, precise, pinpoint casts, but offers a little more distance and latitude than flipping. Pitching is sometimes referred to as long-distance flipping. Pitching is predominantly an underhanded presentation with the reel turned sideways and facing down (Illustration 5.2). Brauer is the master of the loop pitch, which adds a little distance to the normal procedure. Denny's loop-pitch style begins with some two feet of line out from the rod tip, the reel disengaged and the thumb providing a firm brake. Brauer uses his wrist to snap the bait up and around, then releases the thumb bar to let the line out in a normal under-handed pitch. By arching the bait around in a full 360-degree circle before the release, Brauer gains momentum and thus a little extra distance (Illustration 5.3). It's a technique that takes

Illustration 5.1 *Step 1: Let out the amount of line needed to reach the target. With the hand not holding the rod, grasp the line and pull back about half the length* (upper left).

Step 2: Swing the flipping lure back under the rod by lowering it quickly and raising the rod tip (upper right).

Step 3: When the jig starts forward, raise the rod tip and move the rod hand forward to increase the lure speed. At the end of the swing, give a gentle flip to the rod (lower left).

Step 4: As the jig approaches the target, allow the line to slip through your fingers but do not let go of the line completely. Stop the jig just over the water surface (lower right).

some practice, but that's the secret to flipping-and-pitching success. You've got to spend a considerable amount of time developing right-on-target precision. Do that, the pros say, and you'll begin to understand why Denny Brauer wins a lot of big bucks catching bass.

Brauer decided to concentrate on flipping and pitching because he felt it was a real high-percentage technique. The Missouri pro felt like it was a technique that would allow him to

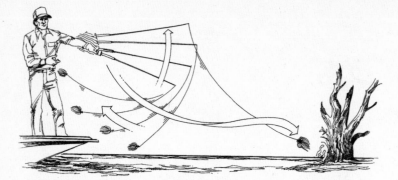

Illustration 5.2 *Pitching is long-distance flipping. The lure, or line just above the lure, is held in the angler's hand and released as the rod swings forward. Unlike flipping, the reel is kept in free-spool position. The weight of the lure pulls line from the spool, allowing for a much longer cast.*

catch larger fish and be competitive as a pro. Other techniques might be more enjoyable to some, but clearly not as effective for catching big fish. The reason Brauer gives for why he developed the flipping-and-pitching techniques as his strong point: "Because I thought it gave me better odds than the other techniques."

SPECIAL TOOLS FOR A SPECIAL TRADE: BRAUER REVEALS THE LONG AND SHORT OF IT

Brauer prefers a 7½-foot-long special flipping-and-pitching rod with a tip action light enough to allow casting-distance and line control. He feels that the soft tip action also helps cushion the hookset when he's flipping into heavy cover, resulting in fewer breakoffs. At the same time the rod contains plenty of backbone, enough to muscle bass out of the wicked underwater structure that flipping and pitching was designed to explore. Brauer likes a single rod that will work for both techniques. He

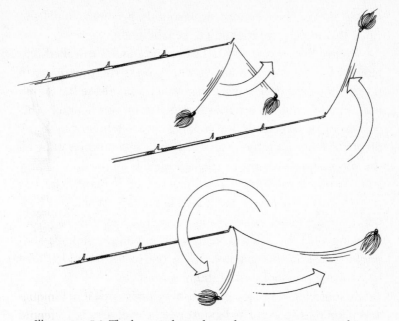

Illustration 5.3 *The loop pitch can be used to gain momentum and in-crease pitching distance. With the reel in free-spool and your thumb pressed firmly on the spool, allow about two feet of line to hang below the rod tip, then snap the lure upward around in a loop. Release your thumb from the spool and allow the force of the lure to carry it forward.*

explains that using one rod for both saves critical time in tour-naments and provides the sort of efficiency that results in more time spent moving the bait in front of more bass. Denny be-lieves that a poor choice of tackle far too often turns frustrated anglers away from these highly productive techniques. The top pitching pro says that beginners tend to choose a rod that's too stiff. He says this results in line breaks or actually tearing the lure out of the fish's mouth. A rod with a softer tip, he says, will work as a shock absorber. He also feels that we're seeing a trend toward flipping-and-pitching rods getting lighter and lighter. This makes them more comfortable for the angler to use. However, he cautions against rods becoming too light, since this impacts your ability to set the hook.

Brauer likes a reel with a fast retrieve and a so-called flipping switch. This switch allows you to press the thumb bar to release line for different distances. When you release the thumb bar, the reel shifts to a retrieve mode for instant hookset. This reel is made especially for flipping and pitching. He keeps plenty of tension on the drag, yet doesn't tighten the setting all the way down. With just a little latitude left on the drag, Denny allows himself room for a small amount of slippage if he sets the hook in what proves to be a truly big fish. When this happens, Brauer wants some give in the reel to keep the bass from breaking off. By using a reel with a built-in flipping-and-pitching feature, he can stop a fish that takes too much drag by applying pressure on the thumb-bar brake.

Brauer believes that a good, heavy line is critical to flipping-and-pitching success. The lightest line he ever uses is 17-pound test. Most of the time he's tied onto a thin-diameter yet extremely strong 30-pound-test monofilament. "If you need light line, then it's probably not a pitching or flipping situation," Brauer points out. "You want a line that will hold up in heavy cover, where fraying quickly becomes a factor. Also keep in mind that you'll need to retie regularly." Denny says that knots fatigue quickly in the heavy flipping-and-pitching lines, so he makes it a practice to retie every time he gets a bait hung up or after every fish he brings to the boat. Denny also feels that a mistake many anglers make is holding the line in their hand when they are jigging the bait. "I see so many guys doing that. They don't want to let go of the line," states Brauer. "When a big bass bites, you have no way to set the hook quickly if you are holding the line."

Another problem Brauer sees is boat control. He says that a lot of anglers are not good at controlling the boat and keeping it at a constant distance from structure, they are too close or too far away, or they are making too much noise.

"Flipping and pitching is an intense way to fish, and it can get complicated," Brauer says. "You can't cut corners if you want to do it right, so make sure you start out with a good rod, line, reel, and that you understand boat control."

And Denny is intense! He relates an experience that his wife, Shirley, will never let him forget. "After weighing in at a major tournament I was really excited," says Brauer. "I wasn't leading, but I was in third and just real pumped up. I took off from the weigh-in, gassed the boat, and went to the hotel. I was working on my tackle when suddenly it came to me, I had left Shirley at the weigh-in. Obviously, I was really into my fishing."

BRAUER ON BAIT:
SPECIAL COMBOS AND COLORS

Then there's the bait. Brauer likes a jig and frog, which remains his big money bait on the pro circuit. Denny usually rigs a ⅜-ounce jig with a #1 Uncle Josh Jumbo Frog. "Remember, a flipping jig needs a strong weed guard and hook," Brauer cautions. "It just isn't the place for light wire hooks, and a lot of top bass fishermen even prefer half- and five-eighths-ounce jigs for both flipping and pitching. As the cover gets heavier, you'll need a heavier jig to penetrate it." Brauer likes his jigs in dark colors, including blue, chartreuse, green, brown, red, and purple. However, his basic jig is black with a few strands of another color added (Illustration 5.4). Some of Denny's best bass-producing combos include a black jig with blue tinsel and a black frog, a black and brown jig with a brown frog, or similar combinations. "You need to figure out colors that work in different water conditions and develop confidence in them," Brauer says. Along with the #1 Jumbo Frog, Denny often turns

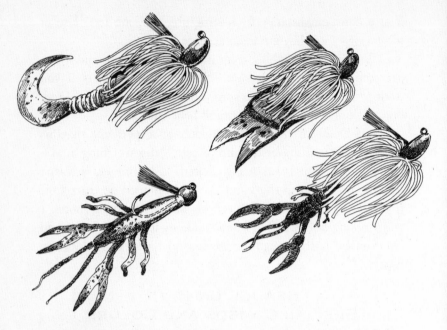

Illustration 5.4 *Denny's favorite flipping and pitching weapons: the dark rubber-skirted jig with a pork-frog trailer (upper right), a dark rubber-skirted jig with a craw worm (lower right), a white rubber-skirted jig with a sickle tail worm (upper left), and a plastic crawfish fished on a plain jig with a fiber weedguard (lower left).*

to a #11 Frog, a #800 Spring Lizard, a #10 Frog, and a #25 Crawfrog.

In warmer water conditions Brauer also likes the plastic crawfish as a trailer. He says that some need to have the length trimmed a little, but that overall, the crawfish can provide some great action. Colors he recommends include black with blue craw, fire and ice, junebug, black with chartreuse craw, and pumpkinseed (Illustration 5.4).

Brauer sometimes flips and pitches worms rigged Texas-style, using a ¼- or ½-ounce slip sinker above 3/0 or 5/0 hook.

Denny uses a toothpick to stabilize the slip sinker. He likes to slide the sinker up the line after inserting the toothpick. Then he trims away any line that may have been frayed or bruised. Next he ties on the hook and rigs the bait.

At other times Brauer does some customizing by removing a jig's rubber skirt and then threading the hook with a plastic crawfish. "This allows you to present a bait with the smaller profile of just the crawfish, and also end up with a little less pressure wave," Denny explains.

Brauer also gets a lot of mileage out of the traditional plastic worm, either as a jig trailer or fished alone.

THE WHITE-JIG SECRET

One of Denny's most productive, but least revealed lures, is a white jig. During certain times of the year, especially summertime, this dynamite secret weapon can outproduce anything else in your tackle box.

Brauer says of the white jig, "When bass are feeding on shad, and that's almost all summer and fall, I think a white jig is like turning on a neon light. First of all, you are matching the shad's color almost perfectly. I'll usually add a white trailer, such as a curly-tail grub. I'll continue to utilize the same size and weight of jig, usually three-eighths to five-eighths of an ounce, with a white rubber skirt. I'll pitch and flip to the same heavy cover, but I'll change my retrieve a lot. Instead of crawling the jig and grub over the heavy cover and letting it fall, I'll swim it through by gently lifting and lowering my rod and pulling the jig forward in a continuous motion." Brauer says an angler should try this different approach as a change of pace. He feels you are sort of "matching the hatch," when bass are feeding predominantly on shad. But don't tell anyone else about this secret!

KEEPING BAITS AND CONDITIONS
IN SYNC

"When the water temperature ranges from forty to seventy degrees, I use a jig and frog," the pro angler points out. "In waters that range from sixty to eighty-five degrees, I go to a jig and plastic craw or worm trailer. From seventy to ninety degrees, I fish the worm by itself." Obviously, there's some temperature overlap, and Brauer says you'll have to experiment and fine-tune your own instincts to select the right bait. However, these ranges offer good starting points.

Denny uses smaller worms in clear water and larger worms in dingy water to create better waves. He cautions anglers to match the hook and sinker size to the size of the worm. "There have been times when I've flipped worms with one-ounce sinkers, just so that I could get the bait down through heavy, matted vegetation," Brauer says. "My favorite worm colors generally coincide with the crawfish colors I like. However, when bass are taking worms and jigs equally well, I'll usually flip or pitch the jig, just because it's a more compact bait and generally fishes a little easier."

BRAUER ON GETTING STARTED:
PRACTICE MAKES PERFECT

Brauer refined his famed casting techniques at home, standing by the couch in front of his television set. "I placed a coffee cup under some house plants on a table. By the end of the winter most of the plants were gone, but I could hit the cup every time," Denny reminisces. The flipping-and-pitching expert stresses that the presentation must be practiced over and over to ensure that it will remain quiet.

"You're primarily dealing with shallow fish," Denny says,

Illustration 5.5 *Denny tries to actually penetrate ambush points with his jig. Most strikes occur as the lure is falling.*

"and the more natural the entry into the water, the better the chances of getting a bite—especially from big bass." So a soft entry is extremely important, and the key is feathering the line just a little right before the bait hits the water. Brauer likes to let his lures fall on a semislack line so that they'll drop straight down into the cover without restriction. At the same time he's always aware of what the baits are doing as they slide down through the water. He says that anytime he can't feel the bait, he sets the hook (Illustration 5.5).

DEVELOPING A SENSE OF FEEL: IT'S PART OF THE BRAUER TOUCH

"It is really important to keep your concentration on the bait and everything that's going on around it," Brauer says. He adds that flippers and pitchers need to watch the cover for any sort of movement. They must also monitor the bait. "You need to know if the bait hits bottom or if something stops it in the process," Brauer says. "You need to know if some brush or reeds suddenly begin to shake when you make your presentation. If you've made a good presentation, this most likely means that a fish has moved to your bait. If it was a bad presentation, then you probably spooked the bass."

Brauer doesn't dwell on finesse when it's time to "check" for a fish. Instead he drops the rod tip, takes a couple of cranks on the reel to pull up some slack, and then sets the hook— hard. "If you think there's a fish on, normally they have the bait and this method keeps them from feeling you and spitting the lure out," Brauer says.

He adds that he does exactly the same thing when he senses that the bait has stopped short of the bottom. If the lure drops freely all the way down, Brauer gives it a couple of pumps and then reels the bait back in for a new cast at some likely looking bass cover. There's little time wasted actually working the bait, since in flipping and pitching the majority of strikes come during the initial drop.

On the other hand, cold water or bad weather conditions can change the slate completely. Brauer says there have been times when he shook a jig in a bush for at least a couple of minutes before a bass bit. He adds that it helps to have a good idea that a fish is holding in the cover if you decide to devote that much time to any one particular cast.

FIND THE RIGHT COVER, FISH IT WITH SKILL

To sums things up, Brauer says that skill and the right kinds of cover are the keys to flipping-and-pitching success. If you're in sparse cover and clear water, try something else. If you've found heavy cover with stained or muddy water, get out the flipping and pitching pole. Denny adds that if the cover is heavy enough, bass usually won't spook if you move in close to flip or pitch a bait. Keep in mind that you'll need to stay off the fish a little bit more if the cover is slim or the water clear: this is where pitching skills come in handy. "If the cover is fairly uniform, I usually flip," Brauer says. "If the cover is scattered or isolated, I like to pitch. Ideal flipping cover might be a long line of grass or reeds that you work with a lot of flipping action, with one cast right after the other. But if you see fish starting to spook, it might be best to back away and pitch."

A FINAL WORD OF WISDOM

Brauer stresses that a quiet approach is mandatory. "Ease your boat up to the cover, or take advantage of wind drift. Do whatever it takes to sneak up on spooky fish," he says. "Most anglers fail to do this."

And last but not least, Denny urges anglers to never give up on a good spot. "I've seen fishermen take a fish off a piece of cover, then race off to the next place," he points out. "When they do that, there's a good chance they've pulled away from more good fish."

Brauer remembers one tournament where he caught five bass over five pounds off of one stump. "I caught two the first time I fished it, then I came back later and caught two more," the flipping-and-pitching king recalls. "Then I came back a third time and caught the final fish."

Zell Rowland has become known nationwide for his
ability to catch bass on a topwater lure.

6

ZELL ROWLAND

*If the Lure Floats, He Loves to Fish It
Better Than Anyone Else*

Catch just one big bass on a topwater bait and you're hooked for life, because few forms of freshwater sportfishing provide so much excitement.

Even so, most anglers view topwater fishing as the stepchild for special occasions: calm water, early or late hours, warm temperatures, shallow bass. Many tournament pros consider the technique to produce smaller fish and to be effective only in these specific circumstances. This attitude has prevailed and explains, to a degree, why many pros spurn topwater.

That's been the book on topwater . . . unless you've heard the bass-fishing gospel according to Zell Rowland. Zell's been cashing bass-tournament checks on the

ZELL
ROWLAND
CONROE, TEXAS

*Holder of three
national bass-fishing
titles. Eight-time BASS
Masters Classic
Finalist. Super
Invitational Bass
Champion. Winner of
bass fishing's biggest
purse, the $175,000
Red Man Diamond
Blend Invitational.*

strength of his topwater techniques for a number of years and throughout a long string of appearances in the famed BASS Masters Classic. At the end of nearly three decades of hard amateur and professional fishing, the Texas angler continues to use floating baits almost exclusively to remain among bass fishing's elite. The highlight of Zell's career to date has been winning pro bass fishing's largest purse, the $175,000 first-place money for the Diamond Blend Championship.

TOPWATER TECHNIQUE: IT'S A WORK OF ART

Zell likes to point out that just about any fisherman can flip a worm around a bush or a boat dock, just as anyone can cast out a crankbait and reel it over some hidden underwater drop-off.

But topwater fishing, the Texan stresses, is like an artist painting a picture. Not everyone can do it, because of the time involved in learning the technique. A topwater lure usually has no built-in action. It is up to the angler to impart the action to the lure. This takes a little time to develop, but also allows the angler to be creative and to experiment. Zell doesn't think very many anglers, amateur or pro, take time to learn how to present topwater baits effectively. If they did, he points out, then more fishermen would discover what a dynamite bass-catching tool they can be!

ON THE TOURNAMENT TRAIL IN HIS TEENS

Rowland was born in Memphis, Tennessee, where he started fishing when he was eight years old. Five years later the young angler entered his first pro B.A.S.S. tournament, back before age limits put a lid on pint-sized participation.

Then Zell's family moved to Texas, where he still makes his home. Those early years were idyllic because the Rowlands were a fishing family. Zell's father still holds a saltwater record, and the Rowland bunch fished everywhere they could wet a line: offshore, on area lakes, from the banks of local stock ponds. And that's how bass fishing got a lasting and lucrative grip on Zell's varied outdoor interests.

Rowland fed his competitive appetite at various local club tournaments after his presence in that first B.A.S.S. tournament led to age sanctions. In a few short years his tackle had grown from cane poles and spincast reels to the 14-karat-gold baitcast reels and custom-made rods he used in competition—a birthday present from his supportive parents.

The desire to become a pro fisherman grew throughout his high school years, and by the time he graduated, there was no question about what Zell Rowland would do to make a living. He turned pro without a backward glance and, encouraged by bass-fishing legends such as Rick Clunn, grew into one of pro bass fishing's superstars, mainly on the strength of his famed topwater technique.

"I'm asked dozens of times a year by anglers, 'How do you get started as a pro?'" Zell says. "Well the answer is, 'Very slowly!' It really gets tougher every year. There are a lot of good young anglers out there. I advise them to fish local and regional bass tournaments to see if this is really for them. If you can win in that environment, on a regular basis, you just may be able to compete as a pro in a professional situation. Once you make that step to the top level, the competition increases tenfold." Zell always advises anglers not to quit their day job! He says that many anglers think that it would be great to fish for a living. Zell admits that it is great, but it comes with a lot of pressure to perform and succeed. "I make it a full-time job," states Zell. "I try to put the time, effort, and energy into striving to make myself a better angler every day."

TOPWATER FISHING: A LABOR OF LOVE

Zell says he concentrated on topwater baits because he simply loves to catch bass on a surface bait. "There's nothing more exciting than watching a fish hit a topwater lure," Rowland says. "It's nothing at all like flipping a jig into a bush where you only see your line jump or the bush shake. With topwater you actually see the fish come up and try to take the lure away from you. That's why I love to catch bass on a surface bait."

TOPWATER'S MORE VERSATILE THAN YOU THINK

Zell also keeps right on fishing his floaters long after other pros have gone back to the tackle box for something that runs a little deeper. "Most people put their topwater lures away when the sun gets real bright," Zell says, "but that's when I tie on another one." Rather than giving up on topwater, Rowland urges anglers to change the size of their bait. Either that or modify how fast or slow they've been working it. "Let the fish tell you what to do," he cautions. It's not unusual for Zell to use topwater baits to catch bass in as much as thirty-five to forty feet of water, a situation where most pros quickly close their tackle-box lids on the floating lures.

MR. MODIFICATION: ZELL AND THE POP R'

Rowland is famous for resurrecting a discontinued lure, the Pop R'. This chugger-type lure was introduced by PRADCO in the early 1980s. The lure didn't sell. It was not that there was anything wrong with the lure, it was just that it was similar in looks to other lures already out there. Everyone had a Heddon Chugger in their tackle box, and the Pop R' looked almost like it except for some Mylar tied on the back treble hook. Zell acquired a Pop R' and was immediately impressed with the lure. He soon discovered that another top pro, Rick Clunn, had been using the lure with great success. PRADCO discontinued the lure, and Zell began going from tackle shop to tackle shop buying up the last existing stock of Pop R's.

As he always does, Zell began to fiddle with the lure, changing this and modifying that. Taking the regular bait (the smallest of the three baits offered today), he removed the hooks and began to sand the lure down to the base. He continued sanding, reshaping the lure to a leaner profile. He sanded the edges of the Popping Chamber (the bowl-shaped front of the bait) until they were very sharp. Removing the factory dressing on the back hook, he tied on four white chicken hackles. He loved the results. This new modification caught bass left and right.

Zell left some of his sanded Pop R's natural bone color, and he also experimented with painting these newfound treasures. He graduated from model paints and a brush to a small spray gun. Today he has a taxidermist paint lures for him.

When the word got out, and it always does, on the success Zell was having with the Pop R', other pros began to use them. This was followed by mainstream demand for the bait, and PRADCO reintroduced the lure. The reintroduced Pop R' was designed to look more like the ones Zell modifies. Now the Pop R' is a topwater standard and comes complete with Zell's autograph on each lure. "The Pop R' will catch bass just the way it comes out of the box," Zell claims. "But I like my modified ones better." As you can imagine, the pressure on Zell to sell these handmade gems comes from all sides. Generally, though, Zell produces just enough of these modified baits for his own use and for his close friends. Zell spends about two hours working on each bait before it meets his specifications. Other lures that fit into this same "popper" bait classification are Storm's Chug-Bug, Heddon's Chugger, and the Japanese lure called a Splash-it.

IT TAKES STYLE TO DO IT RIGHT

Zell likes to create different cadences when he fishes the Pop R', and he urges beginners to remain open-minded about the many ways floating lures can be presented. "Don't just throw the bait out into the water and then jerk it," Rowland emphasizes. "You need to experiment with a variety of cadences in order to draw up a strike, and it's essential to practice your entire repertoire of retrieves as often as possible." Zell says that even now he continues to experiment with various topwater techniques. "In fact I sort of let the fish tell me how they want the bait presented to them," he says. "You never know if you need to jerk the lure two or three times or just throw it out there and jerk once. These are the things you can only figure out by going fishing."

COLORS: KEEP IT NATURAL

Rowland's a big fan of the basic bone color for topwater lures, a shade he says has produced big bass since the 1950s. He'll also modify or match lure color to the prey he finds in the lakes he fishes. "In some lakes you'll see lots of little green minnows, so I throw a green bait," Zell says. "Other lakes may have more shad, and in that case I go with a bait that is chrome-colored. Mostly I try to match the lure to the baitfish in the reservoir."

Rowland prefers hackle feathers on the trailing treble hook of his Pop R', rather than the nylon fibers that most lure man ufacturers now utilize. He says that the feathers seem to "breathe" in the water and entice a strike, while man-made fibers waterlog and produce little or no action.

MAKE YOUR PRESENTATION MEET THE DAY

As a very general rule of thumb, Zell will fish his Pop R' faster in clear water, slower when the water's murky or the day is overcast. When he's really crankin' the lure back to the boat, the bait will throw up a waterspout and make a sound much like a shad breaking the surface.

When he's fishing fast in clear water, the Texas pro usually keeps his rod tip high. When he slows down in stained water or on cloudy days, Rowland may either start with the rod tip low to the water or begin with the tip high and then bring it down or up as the lure approaches the boat. If the slow retrieve doesn't bring results, Zell increases speed.

"I also try to make the lure change sounds as much as possible," Rowland says. "The object is to call fish up to the bait by varying the speed the lure is traveling as well as the noise it makes. An angler should go to a lake or pond, lay out all your topwater baits, and fish each one just to get a feel for the different actions," advises Zell. "Ninety percent of today's fishermen have not even tied on all the lures in their tackle box. Not only does a fisherman need to know his equipment and what all these baits do, but he needs to see their action on light line and heavier line. Don't wait until you are on a dream bassin' vacation to practice with these lures. Know what each does and how to work it. There are a whole lot of good topwater lures out there. This chapter is just going to touch on a few of my favorites."

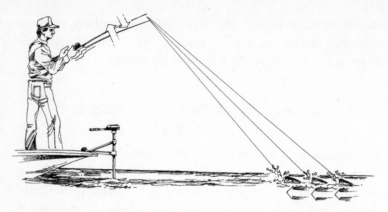

Illustration 6.1 *By holding the rod tip high, the Pop R' can be made to spit and scurry across the surface, imitating a fleeing baitfish.*

Zell ties an improved clinch knot directly to the Pop R', as he does with all the topwater lures he fishes. He does not use a snap. By holding the rod high, Zell can make this lure run and spit like a feeding shad (Illustration 6.1). By lowering his rod tip near the water and reeling slowly while producing quick jerks of the rod, Zell can make the Pop R' chug and walk back and forth, with the front of the bait throwing water with each movement (Illustration 6.2).

WINNING ANGLERS STAY WITH THE FISH

The topwater expert cautions beginners never to give up on a fish. "Sometimes bass will follow a bait all the way to the boat before they hit," he points out. "If the fish strikes when you're pulling the lure out of the water, drop it right back down beside the boat and swish it around. Lots of times bass will come right back around and take it."

Illustration 6.2 *With the rod tip held low and by intermittently jerking the rod and reeling in slack line, the Pop R' will chug and walk left, then right.*

ZELL ON TACKLE:
A LIMBER ROD DOES THE TRICK

Tackle plays a key role in the Zell Rowland style of topwater fishing. Zell likes a high-speed, low-profile baitcast reel. However, he says, it's the rod that really makes a difference. "A good topwater rod needs to be limber," Rowland says. "If the rod is too stiff, the hookset becomes too fast—you'll pull the bait away from the fish." Zell relies on a rod with an extremely limber tip. "A limber rod lets the fish pull the bait down into the water and slows your reaction time a little," he points out. "When you're fishing topwater, you don't want to feel the fish bite the bait. You want to feel the fish when it pulls on the bait. That's why you need a rod that will load up, like a bow and arrow."

Rowland uses monofilament line ranging from 14-pound test for clear water up to 20-pound test if conditions are a bit murkier. He also depends on 17- to 20-pound-test line when

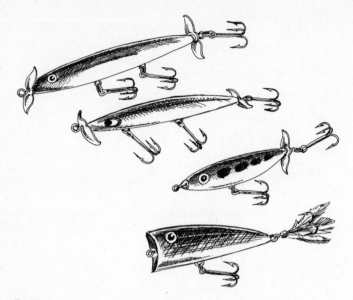

Illustration 6.3 *Four of Zell's favorite topwater lures are* (top to bottom) *the Boy Howdy, the Devil's Horse, the Dalton Special, and of course the Pop R'.*

fishing walking baits, because the heavier lines float, and help with the presentation.

Zell usually leans toward a medium-sized bait, but will go larger or smaller in an instant when he's attempting to devise a fish-producing pattern.

PROPELLER BAITS

Rowland turns to propeller baits when he wants to create a major disturbance on the water's surface. Lures with two propellers, such as the Boy Howdy and the Devil's Horse, tend to retrieve in a straight line, he says. Single-prop styles, such as the Dalton Special, often have a side-to-side action (Illustration

6.3). Zell usually modifies prop baits to suit the needs of the moment. If he wants the lure to move through the water fast, he'll bend the propellers back a bit. If he wants to slow the lure down, then he bends the blades forward.

Most bass fishermen cross off windy days and leave their topwater lures at home. "I never leave my floaters in the tackle box, even if it's windy," Rowland counters. He says that anytime the water temperature climbs to around 55 degrees, he'll be using some type of floating bait.

If he's fishing a strong wind, Rowland may even reverse the hardware so that the front becomes the back and the bait casts into the breeze a little bit better. "Mainly I want the bait to make a disturbance like a shad or bluegill that's been injured," Zell says. "I may start out by working the lure slow, then speed up considerably. At the same time I'll vary what I'm doing with the rod tip so that the bait is always doing something different in the water."

Rowland often uses propeller lures like buzzbaits, fishing them fast across the surface with a steady retrieve. "All in all, you've got to keep the bait moving," he says. "That's the most important factor."

WALKING BAITS: A DIFFERENT NAME FOR A WORLD-CLASS LURE

Walking baits can be a challenge, according to the Texas Classic contender. There are a variety of sizes and models. Each one "walks" differently, and few sound alike in the water. The old standby in this topwater division is the Zara Spook. Others include the Luhr-Jenson Woodwalker and numerous others.

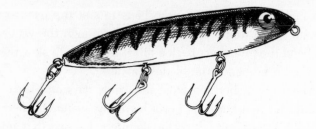

Illustration 6.4 *Zell removes the hooks from his Zara Spooks, reattaching them to the bait, using split rings. This results in free-swinging hooks that won't lock up and pull out when a bass applies pressure.*

First of all, Rowland changes out the hooks on his walking baits, switching to bronze-colored brands that offer less reflection. At the same time he changes the eyelets that attach the hooks to the body, by attaching a split ring to the eyelet and then reattaching the treble hook, resulting in free-swinging hooks that won't jam in place and pull out when the jaw of the fish applies leverage (Illustration 6.4). Sometimes he'll even bend the tie-on eye to the left or right to make the bait walk in a single direction, for example always toward some stationary structure such as a boat dock (Illustration 6.5). Zell asserts that when fished correctly, these lures can pull bass up out of deep, clear water. "If I find a wad of bass on a point, I'll park the boat out in maybe thirty or forty feet of water and cast over the fish," he says. "Then I'll make a big commotion with the bait and pull them up from ten feet or so off the structure." He's seen entire schools of bass come up after the lure in these situations, sometimes as many as ten or fifteen at a time.

"When you fish walking baits, you have to create action with the rod tip. You do it by throwing some eight to ten inches of slack line back at the bait in a synchronized pat-

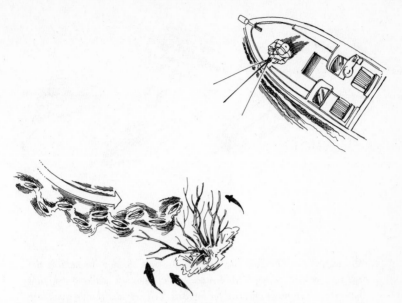

Illustration 6.5 *By bending the front eye of the Zara Spook, you can make the lure walk toward cover. Here, the lure is walking left toward submerged brush.*

tern," Zell points out. Sometimes he stops the bait for a while on overcast days. On bright days he tends to keep the lure moving (Illustration 6.6).

Rowland fishes walking baits with his rod tip high if he wants to keep the nose of the bait pointed up. He lowers the rod tip when he wants the lure to ride level in the water. His presentation is predicated upon long casts. At times he'll only move the lure three or four feet after it hits the water, then slow the action down to a standstill.

"Whatever you do, don't stop the bait when a fish strikes the bait and misses it," the topwater pro stresses. He says

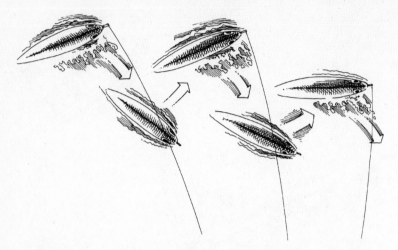

Illustration 6.6 *The Zara can be made to "walk the dog" by holding the rod tip low and jerking. This creates a right, then left, walking style that has proven extremely effective for big bass. Zell actually throws slack line back toward the lure with each jerk.*

that's a common error, one that even haunts seasoned pros due to the excitement of a surface strike. Just keep working the lure and many times that fish will come back and really slam it.

NEW TRENDS
FOR AN OLD LURE

Zell says that there will be many new topwater lures introduced in the near future. Since he works closely with the PRADCO company developing these new lures, he should know. The company will release one or two of these new baits each year. PRADCO has enough new bait ideas, with the popper alone, to produce new lures for the next ten years. These new baits are slightly different from what you've seen in the past, regarding shape, action, and the sounds they create. Zell admits that most of the new lures will not be revolutionary in design. Most are modifications of existing baits. It usually takes a successful old bait to make a new lure.

WHERE TO FISH
TOPWATER LURES

Zell will fish topwater from the first warming of the water in the spring until the frigid chill of winter. Zell explains, "Of course I fish all the other techniques as well, but I always have a topwater rod ready for action." Listed below are Zell's topwater spots season by season.

EARLY SPRING

When the water warms to over 50 degrees, topwater action will be best in the warmest water you can find. This will generally be in the north covers of most lakes. These areas have been protected from the cold north winds, and the sun has been shining on this quiet water, warming it slightly. If there are a number of warm days in the early spring, the surface water of the lake will warm up quickly. If you get a south breeze, the warmer water will be pushed across the lake and it piles up in these north coves. Another spot where warm water will accumulate, in the early spring with a south wind, is the rocks that line a bridge, dam, or railroad trestle. Bass in these areas will be most active. Fish your topwater baits in these areas *very slowly*. You should fish right against the bank. Also, concentrate on cover out to about eight feet deep.

SUMMER

As the water warms, the bass move into a summer pattern. Fish the shallow brush and grass early in the morning and late in the evening. Move out to deep points and shaded boathouses as the day goes on. However, if the water is dingy, or there is cloud cover, you can fish topwater shallow all day long, as the bass have a tendency to remain very shallow.

FALL

Fish all the summer patterns in the fall. You can also move up the creeks to follow the shad each fall. These are general patterns. Bass don't always follow the rules. Zell says that he has caught them in July and August at high noon in two feet of water, so an angler shouldn't get too locked into absolutes when going bass fishing.

IT ALL ADDS UP TO ADRENALINE

And yes, the excitement never completely fades away, even after a quarter century of professional bass fishing. Fellow fishermen still kid Zell about the time he was headed for Lake Mead near Las Vegas, Nevada, and left his boat in the desert. "It was early in the morning," Zell remembers, "and I'd driven about thirty-five miles. You could see the lake in the distance, and I'd just been bragging to a passenger about how well my van was pulling the boat up the hills. Then I glanced in the rearview mirror and realized there wasn't any boat." In his haste to get to the tournament, Zell forgot to latch the trailer down tight. The result was a boat that resembled bomb fragments, out there beside a cactus-studded highway. And a pro fisherman left high and dry.

Then there was the time that Zell swamped a brand-new boat he'd just borrowed down on Lake Sam Rayburn in Texas. Folks say that by the time they dragged the remains out of the water, you couldn't tell that shiny new bass boat from the beach.

I guess that's why Zell Rowland truly is a bass-fishing legend. Definitely on topwater. And sometimes, if you believe all the stories, also under it.

David Fritts has changed the way almost everyone fishes crankbaits.
The "Fritts Blitz" has led anglers away from the shoreline to search out
midlake bass holding structure.

7

DAVID FRITTS

King of the Crankbait Fishing Pros

D avid Fritts says that crankbait fishing is a lot like
having your fingers on the pulse of
a telegraph line. Except in this
case, it's the vibrations of the lure,
transmitted through a few dozen
feet of monofilament, that com-
municates what fishermen need to
know about how and where the
bass are hanging out.

And you can be sure that
when Fritts talks about crankbait
technique, wise anglers listen. After all, this is the guy who burst
onto the pro bass tournament
scene in 1989 and shot straight to
the top. By 1993 David had a
Classic Tournament victory under
his belt. In 1994 he was named
Angler of the Year and vaulted into
the ranks of bass fishing's superstars. And he did it in a way that

DAVID FRITTS
LEXINGTON, NORTH
CAROLINA

*1994 B.A.S.S. Angler
of the Year. 1993
BASS Masters Classic
Champion. Four-time
BASS Masters Classic
Finalist. As 1994
Angler of the Year, he
caught 432 pounds 7
ounces of bass. He also
set a new B.A.S.S.
record for a four-day
event (five-bass limit
each day) of 91 pounds
3 ounces.*

any hardworking novice can master. Fritts is a crankbait fisherman, pure and simple. He fishes the baits you'll find in abundance at tackle stores coast to coast. Diving baits, suspended baits, rattling baits; the "plugs" that millions of kids have coveted over the years, lures made to look and act like minnows, frogs, crawfish, and other natural items in a food chain that big bass relish.

THE BEST WAY TO FISH A CRANKBAIT IS THE WAY YOU START OUT: PLAIN AND SIMPLE . . . BUT YOU MAY WANT TO CUSTOMIZE IT FIRST

Fritts has converted a common and popular form of bass fishing into wads of cash, and he's done it plain and simple, without smoke and mirrors and voodoo techniques. In fact David will tell you that any well-crafted crankbait, straight out of the box, fished without any frills and with a simple, steady retrieve, will put plenty of big fish in the boat. However, David has developed his own method for weighting crankbaits that he feels gives him that extra edge. (More on this later.)

STARTING OUT

The David Fritts story got its start in Lexington, North Carolina. That's where the crankbait king was born, and David has continued to live within five miles of his boyhood home throughout his adult life. Fritts can recall fishing expeditions dating back to when he was six years old. David and his mother were the anglers in the family, and Mom would escort her son to area lakes and creekbanks where they'd catch bass, bream, carp— "anything that would take a bait," David remembers. "Every fish I caught thrilled me to death."

In 1981 David entered his first major bass tournament and won it outright. "It was a local tournament with about four hundred and fifty boats, and I was really fortunate," Fritts remembers. "I'd always dreamed about fishing the pro bass circuit, and winning that first competition gave me a great big confidence boost. That's when I began to think I could actually compete and make a living."

THE KEY TO CRANKBAITS:
COLOR AND COVERING LOTS OF WATER
AT A VARIETY OF DEPTHS

David sticks to crankbaits because he believes the lures allow him to cover large areas of water, explore a variety of depths and then quickly figure out where fish are holding. Fritts also likes the fact that crankbaits duplicate major links in the food chain, such as small sunfish, crawfish, or shad.

Once he's on fish, the North Carolina legend doesn't waste much time on frills. "Mostly, I want to get a bait in the water. I just cast it out and reel it back in," Fritts says. "Sometimes I may vary the speed of the retrieve depending on water temperature. At other times I may use a stop-and-go presentation, or maybe just a pause." However, the crankbait pro doesn't get too carried away with this part of his technique. Fritts likes to point out that when he first started fishing, just good, steady cranking always worked, and it still does today.

On the other hand, David believes that bait color makes a definite difference. "I like crawdad colors in the spring, shad colors in summer, and chartreuse in both summer and fall," he says.

BIG BAITS, SHARP HOOKS, AND LINE
THAT WON'T STRETCH

Fritts also prefers baits in the bigger versions with the large diving bill. "I use three-inch baits mostly, because I like catching fish out of water twelve to eighteen feet deep, and it takes a big crankbait to get down to that depth," the Classic champion points out. "The resulting deep-water hooksets won't present a problem," Fritts adds, "as long as you consistently use extra-sharp hooks and a good brand of line that's not prone to stretch."

KEYING TO THE SEASONS

The pro superstar uses his crankbaits like a probe, searching for fish by feel and with the knowledge he's gained on the B.A.S.S. circuit. "My approach varies according to the part of the country I'm fishing and the type of lake I'm in," Fritts says. "But most of the time in the spring you'll be after staging fish up in coves, creeks, on the big flats, or maybe even on some type of rocky structure. [Staging fish are those bass that move up and hold, usually at the first drop to deeper water, before moving in to spawn.] That's when crawdad patterns really work well."

Later, during the postspawn season, Fritts says he'll look for fish in the same areas—"except then they're moving out toward deeper water, rather than moving in." He fishes for summer bass over deep structure, usually at the mouths of creeks or out in the main body of the lake.

KEYING BAITS TO WATER COLOR

Fritts says that autumn is one of the easiest seasons to fish crankbaits, and that's when he works as much water as possible up in the creeks. The crankbait pro uses the same approach no matter how dirty the water may be, although he's been known to switch to a rattling bait if the water is really dingy, or sometimes even a darker color. In extremely clear water, Fritts often finds it necessary to change to a smaller lure.

TACKLE

Fritts's preference in tackle is also modest. He uses a top-of-the-line 6- to 6½-foot crankin' rod and a baitcast reel with a good, smooth drag. He also feels that the rod should have a fairly soft tip. The North Carolina pro likes a 4.3:1 gear ratio, which he says is ideal for fishing crankbaits, although it's a much slower retrieving reel than most pros use. His line of choice is 10-pound-test monofilament, designed to eliminate stretch.

THE CRANKBAIT KING'S FAVORITE BAITS

Fritts carries tackle boxes crammed full of crankbaits of all descriptions. Yet when it comes to the basics, he likes a bait with a bill built straight into the body, resulting in extremely tight action and a diving depth in the fifteen- to eighteen-foot range.

His favorite deep bait is a Poe's 400 crankbait. He customizes the lure by using a ³⁄₁₆ drill bit and drilling a ½-inch deep hole at about a 45-degree angle between the front hook and where the bill exits the bait at the front of the body. He wraps a piece of electrical tape around the drill bit to assure that he drills no deeper than ½ inch. He uses a drill press and holds the lure in his hands. He does it all by sight and estimates the angle that he wants the hole drilled. When the bit reaches the tape he knows the hole is ½ inch deep. Then he pours melted lead into the hole right up to the top. He finishes the job by applying Epoxy glue over the lead to hold it in and to keep water from soaking into the bait. The finished product sits nose-down on the surface of the water. It will dive deeper and will suspend when you stop the retrieve. Some baits do not suspend perfectly but will very slowly float upward when the retrieve is stopped. At times either of these actions can be extremely effective.

Illustration 7.1 *David Fritts prefers the deep-diving Poe's 400 crankbait, which he customizes by drilling a ³/₁₆-inch-diameter hole ½ inch deep into the lure as shown. He then fills the hole with lead and covers the lead with epoxy glue. David likes a lure with a square-bill, fixed to a 45 degree angle, for shallow water application.*

You can achieve somewhat the same action by applying the new Storm weighted stick-on dots to the lure. Just stick them on at the same place the hole would be drilled. You may have to stick several on top of each other to get the desired weight.

Another trick David uses is to "fade" the color of crankbaits by hanging them out in the sun for prolonged periods of time. The sun fades the clear lacquer, creating an opaque coating which gives the bait a different look.

His second choice, Fritts says, would be the same bait except in a smaller version—a 2½-inch lure rather than 3 inches, for example. It would work well in water eight to twelve feet deep.

Finally, Fritts makes sure he has a bait with an angled or slanted bill, one that produces a lot of vibration, possibly one that includes some type of rattle and runs from five to eight feet deep (Illustration 7.1).

CRANKBAITS AND WEATHER

The crankbait pro doesn't mind inclement weather. In fact, Fritts feels that changing or rough weather conditions are more of a help than a hindrance. "The only problem is that I usually fish structure in the middle of the lake, and sometimes high winds can keep you from getting there," Fritts says.

In calm weather his approach is a little more subtle. That's when he prefers a bait without a rattle, softer colors, and a presentation that drives the lure a little bit deeper.

When a strong weather front approaches, Fritts finds that bass tend to be more aggressive. Then he'll use a rattling version of a bait that's proven successful on the fish or structure he's working, and he may crank the lure a little faster.

SEARCHING FOR CRANKBAIT STRUCTURE

Finding deep crankbait structure is the key to bass-fishing success, Fritts-style. David uses the bait itself as his "eyes" when searching for the type of bottom that holds fish. Though you occasionally hear the term *structure* applied to standing timber, blown-down trees, rocks, boat docks, and so forth, in the true sense of the term these items are cover. Structure is loosely defined as changes in variation in the lake floor (Illustration 7.2). This could be midlake humps, a rock pile under the surface, a creek channel, a long point or any change in the lake floor. "At times you can find big breakoffs and similar structure with your electronic gear," Fritts points out. "But still, the crankbait is the key to locating the right kinds of bottoms, and the bait is what I mostly depend on. When I do find promising structure, I may make several dozen casts probing the whole area. I try to fish an area thoroughly. Also, I don't stand up all day like Jimmy Houston. I've been known to sit down and even rest my rod against my foot, to take some of the pressure

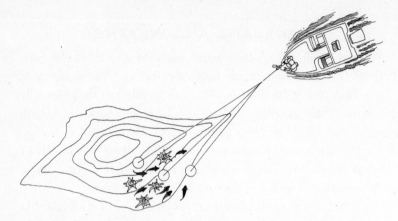

Illustration 7.2 *David will fan-cast a mid-lake hump that drops to deeper water. If he locates stumps, brush, or rocks adjacent to one of these drops, he usually finds bass.*

off my arms and shoulders. If you crank all day, you'll see why."

The former Angler of the Year says it's simply a matter of idling around in the boat, searching for an underwater creek or river channel or maybe a submerged ditch. That's when you start looking for some sort of adjoining cover, usually by casting the crankbait and then "feeling" what happens during the retrieve. Fritts also points out that you can never learn all there is to know about finding offshore structure. "Some anglers see me a quarter mile off shore and think I'm fishing really deep. Many times I'm fishing an eight- to twelve-foot-deep hump or rise in the lake floor. This is the type of structure I'm looking for. If it has cover on it, all the better," claims Fritts.

Therefore, much of Fritts's famed technique is a blend of using electronic aids to help him find the right depth and general fish-holding structure, then more intricate exploration with a lure. "I'm old-fashioned in my approach to fishing, but electronics are fast, dependable, and I know how to use them," the angler points out. "It would be difficult to compete without these special tools. However, most anglers don't have the confidence or the patience to seek out structure and fish it. Some try, but most go back to beating the banks. If you don't really feel like you can catch fish with this technique, then you probably won't."

CRANKBAITS AND SUSPENDED BASS

When Fritts finds suspended bass, he positions his boat so that the crankbait comes right through the area occupied by fish. "You need to make sure that the lure passes through the bass, then abruptly changes directions—either while the bait is still in the middle of the fish or while it's still within eyesight," he emphasizes. The crankbait pro adds that the lure should start rising as it comes through the suspended fish or when it passes beside the school. Either that or you should execute an abrupt angle change, or at least do something dramatically different to alter the presentation (Illustration 7.3).

FINE-TUNING YOUR TECHNIQUE

Fritts also urges beginning crankbait anglers to develop patience. "When I first started fishing, I would leave fish behind," the former Angler of the Year relates. "I would locate fish and start catching them on a certain bait. Then, the next day when the tournament started, I'd return to the same spot. If I didn't get any bites right away, I'd give up and go somewhere else. The fish were still there, but I just didn't have the patience to stay with them. This is one of the biggest mistakes the average angler makes."

Illustration 7.3 *One of David's favorite tricks is to raise his rod during retrieve when he feels the lure is approaching either suspended bass or bass holding on cover. The sudden movement of the lure upward triggers savage strikes.*

Then Fritts began to vary his presentation a little. "I learned to go back to a good spot and try something just a little different if the fish weren't biting, and I began to really wallop the bass," he said. "Don't ever give up on a good spot without a little experimentation—use some different baits and experiment with actions before you leave." He adds that crankbait fishermen too often fail to develop the touch necessary for successfully catching big bass.

"You need to elevate your technique to the point that it feels like you're fishing a finesse bait," Fritts says. "You want to feel every move that lure makes, and you need to recognize when something doesn't feel exactly right down there."

Fritts works hard at his craft, rising early to spend extra hours on the lake. "I always try to find good fish, and I gamble a lot," he says. "A lot of fishermen set their goal at eight or nine pounds of bass a day. I fish to catch twenty pounds a day, no matter where I'm at." His edge, he says, is knowledge gained from long hours of serious fishing. Fritts has developed an extraordinary insight into crankbait technique, and he's learned to make quick adjustments in colors, tactics, and type of bait out on the water where it counts.

The B.A.S.S. circuit superstar chose crankbaits early because, he says, they were the easiest way to fish. "In those early years I could always count on catching bass with a crankbait, because about all you had to do was toss the lure under a tree and reel it back in," Fritts recalls. Early success yielded confidence, and with the confidence came refinements in technique. "It always seemed to me that crankbaits were more lifelike than any of the other baits," Fritts says. "Besides, I enjoy the way you fish the baits. It lets me keep moving and reeling. And that's what I like."

PLAYING THE BASS AND LANDING HIM WITH THE BELLY-LIFT METHOD

The North Carolina pro often gets asked about his fish-landing method. He terms it as sort of an offshoot of the old "belly-lift" method. "When I hook a bass on a crankbait, I play him very carefully," states Fritts. "The soft-tip rod I'm using helps in regard to keeping pressure on the fish, but not ripping the hooks out of his mouth. Most bass lost on crankbaits are lost because anglers try to horse a fish quickly into the boat, usually with a stiff rod." David says that this applies all kinds of pressure to the hooks and they just pull loose. "I'll play the fish until he's tired and attempt to keep him away from the boat," Fritts proclaims. "I try to judge what size fish I have on and plan my landing effort before I get him to the boat. When I get him right alongside the boat, I reach out and try to pin him to the boat with my hand under his belly, away from all those treble hooks." Fritts then says that he "slides his hand under the fish's belly and lifts. They used to say the weight of the fish bearing down on his internal organs caused him to relax. It doesn't hurt the fish in the least." Fritts says that he and Tommy Martin are the only two pros currently using this method. "It works great," David says as he smiles, "if you don't count that one time" (see next section).

ON THE LIGHTER SIDE:
ALL WET

Yet even David Fritts, the crankbait-fishing superstar, isn't totally infallible. There have been times when he's seemed as awkward as a hog on a skating rink, and, like all good southern boys, Fritts has learned to laugh at professional fishing's embarrassing moments and misfortunes.

Once the TV cameras were even on hand to show the world how Fritts, working hard to win a Superstars Tournament in Peoria, Illinois, could get so excited by a big fish that he fell out of the boat attempting to land it. "I was really concentrating on landing that fish," Fritts recalls. "It was a good one, and I needed to catch it in the worst sort of way." The crankbait king had the big bass close to the boat when it made a final lunge away from his grasp. "Well, I leaned over, reached out too far, and got too much of my weight out over the edge of the boat," Fritts relates. In an instant the North Carolina pro was swimming in the river with his catch. But true to form, Fritts wasn't about to give up on a bass that seemed to have dollar signs tattooed all over its scaly green hide. He bobbed to the surface, reeled the bass up to the rod tip, grabbed the fish, and threw it in the boat. Then he tossed his tackle in after the bass and got a helping hand back onboard. All this was caught on camera by a professional television

crew, and Fritts handled the jokes good-naturedly—both during the premiere showing and during reruns. Like he says, "If
you make your living on the water, you're going to get wet."
And wet or dry, David Fritts has made an unbelievably good
living fishing crankbaits for bass!

This 13-pound 3-ounce monster was taken by Rich Tauber on a Gitzit fished on spinning gear with 8-pound-test line from California's Lake Castaic.

8

RICH TAUBER

The Light Touch for Big Bass

When the hard-core bass fishing crowd heard about Rich Tauber and his West Coast finesse approach, most dismissed him as a joke. But soon the southern boys started paying attention, especially when Tauber's light touch brought bass to the boat while traditional methods stalled in the water and the old standards struck out.

Tauber's open-faced spinning reel, reed-thin rod, and nearly invisible light line certainly seemed out of place among a crank-and-grind school that emphasized big lures, heavy tackle, and tough line with the winching power of a tow truck. Yet Tauber remained undaunted, even in the midst of all that early redneck derision, and

RICH TAUBER
WOODLAND HILLS,
CALIFORNIA

*Winner of the $50,000
U.S. Open. Three-time
BASS Masters Classic
Finalist*

stuck to his novel Gitzit tube jigs and light-as-a-feather delivery.

What it did for the bass pro was win tournaments. Soon the traditionalists were also carrying spinning rods in their boats, right there amid the standard classic baitcast tackle and box upon box of big worms, big weights, and high expectations.

Tauber knew he'd finally arrived when he fished a pro B.A.S.S. tournament that featured three hundred contestants. Of those three hundred, exactly half were using a spinning rod for specialized lightweight presentations.

GITZIT FISHING: THE LIGHT TOUCH FOR BIG BASS

It was a big barrier to break, and Tauber claims that the lure, rather than the tackle, is truly responsible for the finesse-fishing craze he helped create. "I knew this was going to be big," Tauber said. "As a matter of fact, finesse fishing has proven to be one of the major bass fishing innovations of the nineties. There's even a move afoot to make finesse-type modifications in a lot of the more traditional techniques. Everything is scaling down."

The Gitzit that helped Tauber make a name for himself is an enlarged version of the tube jig, popular among crappie fishermen. To be exact, it is a hollow plastic tube that fits onto a lead-head hook, specifically a size 2/0 Gamakatzu. The lure looks like a hollow plastic sausage with a long, fringed tail. Tauber prefers the original version invented by Bobby Garland of Utah in 1977. The West Coast angler ties his Gitzits onto clear 8-pound-test line matched with a 6½-foot, medium-action spinning rod and a fast-retrieve spinning reel.

All in all, the Gitzit/spinning-tackle/light-line combo has helped Tauber make a good living in the outdoor field he loves and be recognized as an authority on light-tackle fishing. For the Californian who started fishing when he was just a toddler, it's been a dream come true.

FROM BLUEGILLS AND BOBBERS TO BASS-FISHING INNOVATOR

Rich was born in Illinois, but moved to California at an early age. Tauber learned to fish by walking the banks of little lakes near Santa Barbara, fishing for bluegill with a bobber and cane pole.

Later Rich graduated to bass fishing, and as soon as he caught that first big fish, he knew he was hooked. The young West Coast angler devoured the articles in *Bassmaster* and *Western Bass* magazines, joined a bass fishing club at sixteen, and became a big winner on the western tour two years later.

In 1982, Tauber won the prestigious U.S. Open Tournament on Lake Mead, and the cash reward seemed like a godsend to his career. "Before that prize money I had one hundred dollars in the bank. Afterward I had fifty thousand dollars," Tauber recalls. "It was the boost I needed to seriously compete on the tournament trail."

Since then, Tauber's light touch has taken him to the BASS Masters Classic and kept him in demand as a light-tackle spokesman. However, the real thrill remains the feel of the bass on the end of the line—the anticipation, the excitement, the actual strike, the adrenaline rush as the fish edges ever closer to the boat. "It's one of those sports that you have to actually do to understand," Tauber says. "It's just tremendously addictive."

FINESSE FISHING:
PLENTY OF VERSATILITY
THE TAUBER WAY

Before he discovered the Gitzit, Tauber was mostly a plastic worm fisherman. "I've always tried to concentrate on all types of techniques, but the Gitzit was truly a trendsetting lure. And it is versatile: You can flip it, pitch it, cast it. There are any number of ways for this bait to be effective."

Tauber says he'll turn to a Gitzit-type lure in any water up to ten feet deep, over any structure that holds bass. "The thing you've got to remember," he says, "is that these lures generate strikes due to the way they fall in the water. If you tighten your line or inhibit the action of the lure in any way, you're killing its effectiveness."

The Californian likes colors including salt-and-pepper, smoke with a silver flake, and pumpkinseed with green flakes. "I'll use the lighter colors in darker water or when the bass are keying on shad," he says. "If the fish are eating crayfish, then I'll use darker colors such as the pumpkinseed."

Mostly, Tauber's brand of finesse fishing works best in clear water. He defines clear water as any water you can see through from two to two hundred feet. Thus it is basically a clear-water technique. The bass need to be able to see the bait fall. Tauber says if the water is murky, try something else. Also, while he won't call this technique a last resort, many anglers use it as such. Generally if you can't catch bass on your power lures—spinnerbaits, crankbaits, or big plastic worms—then that's the exact time to go to the Gitzit. "I feel it will catch bass when nothing else will," claims Tauber. "As a result, I use it more than any of the other techniques."

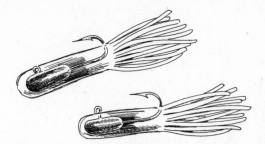

Illustration 8.1 *Rigging a Gitzit with a cylinder-head jig requires that the jig head be inserted through the rear of the tube. When the head of the jig is all the way forward, press down on the plastic around the eye of the hook, forcing it through the plastic.*

THE ACTION THAT DRIVES BASS MAD

Tauber wants the bass to see the action of the bait as it falls. "Most baits drop straight down through the water," he points out. "The Gitzit is the only one I know of that sways or spirals as it drops down. I use a small cylinder jig head so that the bait will start swaying as soon as it enters the water (Illustration 8.1). Actually the lure will rock back and forth two or three feet as it drops, and that's the motion that triggers the strike. Bass just can't stand that kind of action" (Illustration 8.2).

Tauber slips a ¹/₁₆th-ounce jig head into the tube and then pushes the eye of the jig out through the plastic, locking the combination firmly into place. Tauber says the hook must be exactly in the middle of the tube for the lure to sway. If he wants the bait to spiral during the drop, he rigs the hook to the side.

"You can do a lot of little things to give these lures a different action," he says. "Anglers need to experiment, because the way that the tube falls through the water is crucial. The swaying fall is by far the number-one action I try to obtain."

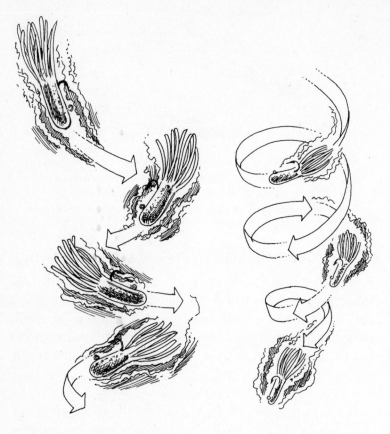

Illustration 8.2 *When rigged, the Gitzit will fall either with a spiraling motion* (right) *or with Rich Tauber's favorite swaying motion* (left).

Tauber did his experimenting during the early days of his career, on California lakes where he could watch the Gitzits drop as much as thirty feet down. "I could always see the fish strike the lure," he remembers. "So I worked on technique by fishing without a hook. Sometimes it was almost impossible to jerk the bait out of the fish's mouth. My rod would bend double and the bass would still be pulling hard."

DEVELOPING THAT LIGHT LURE "FEEL" THAT CATCHES FISH

The Californian says he likes to cast out some twenty to fifty feet, engage the reel, and drop the rod tip toward the bait, leaving the line totally slack, allowing the lure to fall with that classic swaying motion. Then he lifts the line. "If I only feel one-sixteenth of an ounce, I know I don't have a fish," he says. "But if I feel a quarter of an ounce, then I know I've got one." Tauber says that all you have to do is feel that your line is heavier than usual. "Develop that skill and you'll catch fish that most anglers wouldn't catch," he says.

Tauber says that if the bait doesn't produce a strike on the initial fall, then a Gitzit fisherman should begin popping it back to the boat, giving slack line to the lure every time he lifts it off the bottom and allowing it to fall back. "As you get better with this lure, you'll be able to feel what's going on," the West Coast angler says. "You'll sense the amount of slack in the line and be able to see your line pop when you jerk the Gitzit up and toward the boat."

GITZITS: LURES THAT STAND ALONE

Tauber is very emphatic about disassociating Gitzit fishing from plastic worm and jig fishing. "People use Gitzits in colors that have been successful for them in plastic worms," he says. "But the techniques are totally different and the two just don't relate."

Tauber says that many uninformed anglers fish Gitzits with too much weight, mostly because they're conditioned to feeling a lot of weight with other plastic baits. "Adding weight makes the presentation too heavy," he points out. "Sure, you can go out and catch bass on a heavily weighted Gitzit. But what you've done is convert the bait into a lead-head jig. I rarely fish a Gitzit more than twelve to fourteen feet deep, because if you go any deeper than that, the weight is too light to allow much control over the line. If I need to put on a heavier weight, I've made a transformation to a straight sinking lure. So when I need to fish from fourteen to sixty feet deep, I switch to a grub."

When he's in a pure western Gitzit-fishing mode, Tauber usually relies on two stock colors. "I really like salt and pepper and pumpkin and pepper, because they're both good colors in California and Arizona, and ninety percent of my catch there comes on those two baits," he says.

THE GITZIT AND THE GLIDER

Although Rich prefers to fish a Gitzit with an open-hook jig, he will at times use a cylinder-head jig with a small wire weed-guard. Under situations where you must swim the lure through brush, rocks, or other cover, he prefers to rig the Gitzit with the Gitzit Glider. The Glider is a small piece of lead resembling a watermelon seed, with a hole at the top of the widest portion. Ted Miller, from Kingman, Arizona, developed the Glider, and its design is ingenious. Tauber suggests that you use a 2/0 Gamakatsu offset worm hook tied to your line. The shape of this hook fits the Gitzit body and holds the Glider weight in place. To rig the Gitzit with the Glider, begin by slipping the weight into the hollow tube of the Gitzit with the hole (in the Glider) at the top of the Gitzit. Push the Glider all the way to the top of the tube and hold it there by squeezing against the sides of the Gitzit. Take the offset hook and insert it directly into the head of the Gitzit. Push the point of the hook into the head of the Gitzit tube the exact distance that the hole in the glider is from the top of the tube (about ¼ inch). Now turn the hook at a right angle and push it through the hole in the Glider. Continue pushing the hook

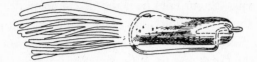

Illustration 8.3 *When rigged with the Gitzit Glider, the Gitzit is virtually snag free.*

straight out through the side of the Gitzit. Now thread your hook out through the side of the Gitzit and continue threading until the offset portion of the hook is inside the tube. The Glider will hang perfectly on the offset portion. The eye of the hook is pulled inside the tube. Next, thread the point of the hook through the tails of the Gitzit, being careful to keep it in the center. The final step is to skin-hook the point of your hook just under the skin of the tube. You now have a nearly snagproof lure (Illustration 8.3). When a fish inhales the Gitzit, and the walls of the Gitzit collapse, this enables you to set the hook easily.

WHEN AND WHERE TO FISH THE GITZIT

Tauber believes that, aside from its being a clear-water technique, early spring and throughout the summer are the best times to fish the Gitzit. "In the fall and winter I use other techniques," says the California pro. "I use the open-hook jig or the Glider, depending on the requirements of the situation." Rich states that both have exactly the same action if rigged properly.

SPRING

In prespawn conditions, Tauber will fish the areas where bass stage before moving into spawn. The pro says that protected cover, with shallow gravel banks, is a likely spot. He also states that fish will stage or hold near the first drop to deeper water, out from these spawning areas. They will also hold on points and around deeper brush. If the area has a hard bottom, Rich will "fall" the Gitzit and jig. If heavy cover is present, he utilizes the Gitzit rigged on a Glider. Here he concentrates on the "slack line" method of presenting the bait.

SIGHT FISHING

When bass actually move up to the spawning beds, Tauber utilizes the Gitzit as a sight-fishing tool. Rich emphasizes that if you fish for spawning bass, it should be a catch-and-release situation only. Any bass caught should be returned to the water immediately. He also stresses that for any sight fishing, a good pair of Polaroid sunglasses are an absolute requirement. "For sight fishing I utilize a different color Gitzit," explains Tauber. "The body of the tube is chartreuse with silver metalflakes. The tails of the tube are clear with silver metalflakes. The color serves two purposes. It's a color that is attractive to the bass and it serves as a strike indicator."

For example, "If I spot a bedding bass, I approach it as carefully as possible," states Tauber. "I keep a low profile, on the front of my boat, usually kneeling. I make a soft under-handed pitch cast and feather the line of my spinning reel with my index finger to achieve an accurate cast and a soft, almost splashless, entry. I will make any number of casts to this fish before the fish responds. Some never do. But the Gitzit is the best lure I know of for catching bass you can see. When the bass takes the lure, if I can see the chartreuse color of the lure, I know the bass doesn't have the lure in his mouth. When the chartreuse disappears, I set the hook."

Rich points out that bedding bass are not the only bass you can sight fish for. He says that there are visible cruising bass, and bass holding on underwater cover, all summer. If you approach them carefully, they can also be caught on a Gitzit.

SUMMER

Tauber says to concentrate on points, and fish more brushy areas in the summer. As a result, he uses the Gitzit rigged with a Glider more, because it is weedless. He also likes to fish boat docks and overhanging cover. "You can skip this lure a good distance under overlapping trees and docks if you do a little practicing," boasts Tauber. He says that the skipping technique actually imitates the minnows you see in the summer, skipping once or twice across the surface before reentering the water. Rich says, "In heavy cover I'll sometimes go to ten-pound-test line, but you'd be surprised how you can lead a bass out of cover, on light line, if you don't apply extreme pressure."

FINESSE FISHING AND THE MIND GAME

Tauber says it also helps to work on mental toughness and concentration. "Good fishermen need to concentrate on what they're doing," he says. "If you're fishing a Gitzit, concentrate on technique, and do it with all the mental toughness you can muster."

The California light-tackle pro adds that instruction and advice are essential to developing the techniques and skills needed to consistently catch bass. "You need to spend as much time around expert anglers as you possibly can," Tauber says. "Take their advice and put it to good use. Learn from their experiences, and be thankful that you had the opportunity to do so."

Tauber feels that too many beginning bass fishermen do the wrong things mechanically. "Most beginners just don't pay enough attention to the basics, the fundamental mechanics that make you a good fisherman," he says. "Work on the nuts and bolts of your presentation, iron out the wrinkles in the way you physically handle the rod, reel, line, and lure. Watch all the videos you can, go to bass-fishing seminars if some are available in your area. Do what it takes to improve and learn. Bass fishing is just like any other endeavor in life. You get back what you put into it."

DESIRE: A KEY ANGLING ELEMENT

The finesse-fishing expert says his tournament successes have been the by-product of two key elements: drive and desire. "When I first started fishing the pro circuit, I was driven by a strong desire to be the best," Tauber said. "I lived and breathed fishing twenty-four hours a day. Now I'm involved in so many other things that it's hard to retain that level of concentration, that level of desire. Yet that's what it takes to excel at first—a true commitment to the sport and the way you participate in it." As it stands, Tauber now excels in several other fields related to the bass-fishing experience. For one, he's an acknowledged expert on light-tackle techniques, eagerly sought after for seminars from coast to coast.

And even though Tauber is generally associated with the West Coast school of bass fishing, he's helped revolutionize the way pros all across the continent now view light-lure presentations. Light lines and spinning tackle are no longer the novelty they once were. More and more pros are branching out, experimenting with Tauber's willow-wand rods and nearly invisible monofilament lines attached to lures that spiral and flutter rather than splash, chug, and sputter.

"There is plenty of room for innovation in the sport of bass fishing, and the techniques we're developing today will be around for generations to come," Tauber says. "I love the sport because it allows you to use your imagination, experiment, and be outdoors at the same time. Bass fishing has been the perfect thing for me to concentrate on, because I never wanted to get a real job anyway."

O. T. Fears has proven that, when it comes to locating concentrations
of bass, nothing works better than the Carolina Rig.

9

O. T. FEARS

When It Comes to Carolina Rigging, This Sallisaw Flash Is on Top of the Game

O. T. Fears is another of the many outstanding Oklahoma bass fishermen who came out of the hills and lakes along the state's eastern border. His hometown is Sallisaw, the place that gave America Pretty Boy Floyd. O.T. may not know much about robbing banks, but when it comes to rigging a bass bait Carolina-style, his reputation ranks right up there with J. Edgar Hoover's Depression-era archenemy outlaw.

Fears learned to love the outdoors from the time he graduated from diapers. He was only four years old when his father and grandparents began to take him along with his brothers and sisters to one of the many creeks that ran through the old Cherokee Nation. Once they'd settled in the shade of

O. T. FEARS
SALLISAW,
OKLAHOMA

1994 B.A.S.S. SuperStars Champion. $100,000 Redman All-American National Champion. Three-time BASS Masters Classic Finalist. A licensed fisheries biologist. He set two new B.A.S.S. records in 1994. For a three-day B.A.S.S. event (five-bass limit) he caught a record 77 pounds 4 ounces of bass. He also set a new one-day (five-bass limit) record of 34 pounds 4 ounces.

some streambank grove, the toddlers would wait patiently for a tug at the tip of the long cane pole pressed firmly between sets of knobby knees, wiggling in anticipation of the fat green "brim" that would soon be flopping at their feet.

The Fears family fished for anything that would bite: catfish, bluegill, bass, it just didn't matter. As O.T. grew older, he learned to use a Zebco spincast reel and some of his grandfather's old baitcast reels. New techniques sprang from the pages of magazines such as *Field & Stream* and *Outdoor Life,* and when the U.S. Army Corps of Engineers began to dam up many of the hill-country streams, Fears traveled to nearby Tenkiller Reservoir on the Illinois River to teach himself big-water techniques for bass.

FROM SMALL TOURNAMENTS TO BIG WINNINGS

Soon O.T. was winning a number of the small local bass tournaments that proliferated during the birth of the bass-fishing craze back in the early 1970s. After a while Fears felt he'd developed a pattern of consistency, a pattern he felt was strong and solid enough to give him a chance to compete in the pro B.A.S.S. ranks. "From the start I loved the challenge of this sport," Fears recalls. "I love to try to meet the challenge and come up with the right answers. Sometimes I do and sometimes I don't."

So the Sallisaw angler turned pro. Today O.T. remains one of the circuit's top hands, a true veteran of a rough and tremendously fickle sport. Fears is also recognized as one of the best Carolina riggers in the field. It's an honor he earned on the water, catching fish and collecting prize money for his winning efforts. While fishing the B.A.S.S. Invitational at Santee Cooper Lake in South Carolina, O.T. established a new weight record for bass caught in one day. The official record was a total weight for a five-bass limit caught in one day of 34 pounds 4 ounces. That is almost a seven-pound average. He also set a new record for a three-day B.A.S.S. event (five-fish limit) of 77 pounds 4 ounces. And he caught most of them on a Carolina rig. So whenever O. T. Fears talks about Carolina rigging, other bass fishermen, even the best, stop to listen. But Fears continued to impress, as he won the B.A.S.S. SuperStars event by switching tactics and claiming that crown by fishing a spinnerbait. He has become the voice of experience, one that demands attention and respect, no matter what the technique.

CAROLINA RIGGING: STYLE AND SUBSTANCE

Carolina rigging, for those who are not familiar with the technique, is a way of fishing a plastic bait such as a worm, lizard, French Fry, craw lure, or Sluggo, to name a few. To rig up Carolina-style, the bass fisherman first threads a ½-ounce, ¾-ounce, or 1-ounce sinker onto the main line on the reel. The sinker can either be a special Carolina-rig brass or lead sinker, or a regular lead-egg sinker. Next you add either a special glass or plastic bead, available at most tackle stores. After this, some anglers prefer to slip on an optional brass disk to add additional click to the rig. Generally, the disk is considered optional. Then comes a barrel swivel.

At this point the angler adds a length of leader material to the end of the regular line. The length of the leader is anywhere from eighteen inches to five feet, with about three feet considered normal. The material is generally another piece of monofilament that's a bit lighter in test than the regular line. For example, if the reel is wound with 20-pound-test line, then the leader may be 15- or 17-pound test. Some fishermen may go all the way down to 10-pound test, especially in clear-water situations. Next comes either a 1/0, 2/0, 3/0, or 4/0 offset hook. Onto this you thread your favorite Carolina-rigged bait. Generally, O.T. rigs with a one-ounce weight unless he's in shallow water or fishing through dense grass. "I like a three-quarter-ounce weight in grass because it's easier to pull it through," he says. However most of the time Fears wants the bigger weight, because it stays in contact with the bottom (Illustration 9.1).

"The weight itself serves as an attraction," O.T. points out. "It scrapes along and creates noise, disturbs the bottom. I believe that fish come to see what all the commotion is, and that's when they see the bait and bite it" (Illustration 9.2).

That's the nuts and bolts of how to Carolina-rig. The art lies in how to fish the rig, and O.T. Fears is a master. Most of the bass pros are turning to Carolina-style fishing because of the tremendous success it presently enjoys. Yet even so, few do it better than the Sallisaw veteran.

RIGGING FOR PRESPAWN AND POSTSPAWN BASS

Fears especially likes to rig up Carolina-style when he's fishing for prespawn and postspawn bass. He feels that the fish aren't clinging tight to the bottom of the lake at these times, the way they may be at other periods when Texas-rigged baits or a jig may be more effective. Yet in that prespawn and postspawn period, Fears likes the fact that his Carolina-rigged bait is up off the bottom when he's fishing for suspended bass. He says that Carolina rigging helps him cover more water and invites quicker bites.

Fears believes that suspended bass just don't key as strongly to structure or the bottom as one might think. He says shallow fish may cling more tightly to structure, but deep fish usually disassociate from structure and suspend off of it. This is not to say that O.T. forsakes his Carolina rigging when he's fishing

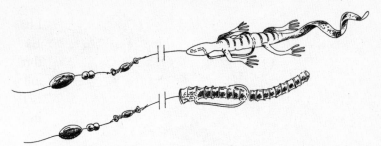

Illustration 9.1 *O.T.'s standard Carolina Rig includes a one-ounce bullet weight rigged ahead of two glass beads and a barrel swivel. A leader of somewhat lesser pound-test than the main line is attached to the barrel swivel and then to a hook to which the plastic lizard is rigged.*

for shallow-water bass. "I've used a Carolina rig effectively in three or four feet of water," Fears says. "You'll need to shorten your leader in shallow water, and I generally won't throw a one-ounce weight in water that's less than five feet deep. In shallow water I switch to a three-quarter-ounce weight."

THE CAROLINA-RIG RETRIEVE

Fears prefers a style of retrieve that involves dragging the weight across the bottom. "If you pull the weight up from the bottom, you're going to get what I call sinker bites," he says. "Sometimes the fish will strike the weight more than they hit the bait that's floating along above it." Although Fears doesn't use it much, he's quick to point out that lately some pros have been using a jig for the sinker. Some are catching a few of those "sinker bites." Looking for future trends, O.T. predicts that we may see some changes in the rig that would allow for creating a louder click and also include a special lure to catch all those "sinker bites." Again, he reminds anglers, "If you want to avoid sinker bites, keep that sinker dragging on the bottom." O.T. says that it's best to let the fish dictate the speed of the retrieve.

Illustration 9.2 *During the retrieve the lizard will rise slightly off the bottom.*

He points out that at times bass won't bite unless the bait remains almost perfectly still. At other times you'll need to move the rig along fairly fast to draw some action. Under most conditions, a slow retrieve works best.

O.T.'s FAVORITE BAITS AND COLORS

Fears's favorite Carolina-rig bait is a six-inch-long salty lizard. However, there are times when the fish won't touch anything other than the small, inconspicuous lure called a French Fry. O.T. says he's Carolina-rigged four- and six-inch worms and even ten-inch lizards. He's even rigged grubs and been successful.

O.T. has definite color preferences in his baits. He likes pumpkin, green pumpkin, and chartreuse, with green pumpkin edging out plain pumpkin as his personal favorite. "Pumpkin has a cinnamon-brown tint, while the green pumpkin has a bit more of a green cast to it," Fears says. "The way I get that green-pumpkin shade is by dipping a regular pumpkin-colored lizard into a green- or watermelon-colored dye."

The Soft Strike

Fears says that fishermen almost never feel the fish take the bait when they're using a Carolina rig. What you eventually feel is the bulk of the fish itself, a sense of dead or mushy weight. Then the bass will swim away with the lure. Sometimes smaller fish may jolt the bait hard, while bigger bass move away with the lure slowly. Sometimes they don't move away at all.

"When I was fishing Lake Santee Cooper, the bass would take hold of the lizard and when I pulled tight against them, the fish just sat there," Fears said. "They never swam away with the bait and they wouldn't move until I set the hook."

The Sweep Hookset

Fears uses a method of hooksetting he calls a sweep set, which involves turning the body at a right angle to the fish and pulling the line to the side rather than the traditional quick elevation of the rod tip. "You want to pull the hook into the fish and cover as much distance with your rod as you can," O.T. explains. "So you keep the rod horizontal to the plane of the water and then turn your body sideways, pulling the rod with you as you do. You can really take up a lot of line fast by moving a seven- or seven-and-a-half-foot rod that much distance."

Let Water Conditions Determine Lines and Colors

In dingy water, Fears uses a pumpkin-colored lizard with a chartreuse tail. Sometimes he'll even switch to straight chartreuse. In clear or slightly stained water, O.T. likes the plain pumpkin, green pumpkin, or watermelon seed, which is green with a black flake. If the sun is shining brightly, Fears may switch to a cotton-candy lizard, a purplish-pink bait with purple and green flakes. "The cotton-candy color seems to work better than just about anything else when the sun is shining," the Sallisaw angler says. "It's more of a translucent color, and the flakes give off a sparkle in the water when the sun shines."

In clear and open water, O.T. turns to a lighter test leader and a smaller-diameter main line. "I may go all the way down to a ten-pound-test leader if the water's clear," Fears says. If he's fishing murky water, O.T. says he'll use a 17- to 20-pound-test leader almost all the time.

TECHNIQUES AND TACKLE

During the early spring months, O.T. concentrates on the main points jutting out into the lake, then on the secondary points leading back into spawning pockets that attract fish. After the spawn, Fears fishes just beyond the breakline out from the spawning banks of the coves, in water that he says is usually from five to ten feet deep.

The Carolina rig expert uses a 7- or 7½-foot rod. His current model is a fairly limber graphite crankin' rod that has what Fears refers to as a lot of bend. "I don't like a really stiff rod when I'm Carolina rig fishing," O.T. says. "I'd rather have one that has some give to it."

Fears prefers a baitcast reel with a 6.2:1 gear ratio so that he can take up slack line faster. His favorite primary line is green 20-pound test with 17-pound test for the leader. In extremely clear water he'll drop to 10-pound test and sometimes go down to 8-pound test when he's fishing for smallmouths.

Some fishermen are fanatics concerning the floating qualities of their lures. But O.T. doesn't think it makes much difference. "We try to get them to float and we generally think floating is better, but I'm not real sure," he said. "Every time you move a Carolina-rigged bait, it will plane up and then settle back down. I think that once the fish come over and check out the commotion, they see the bait planing up off the bottom just a little bit and that's when they grab it. Probably that's why you never feel the bite. The bass swim up to the bait, but they never really attempt to kill it. They just grab hold and swim away."

Fears turns to a smaller bait such as a French Fry on days when the skies are clear and the barometer is high. But if a front is moving in or it's overcast, the Sallisaw fisherman switches back to his favored lizard. He uses a 1/0 hook for a six-inch lizard and will sometimes use a 2/0 depending upon the size of the bait. French Fry–sized baits are presented on 1/0 and even size 1 hooks.

SLOW THAT RIG DOWN!

O.T. cautions anglers not to fish a Carolina rig too fast. He says too many novices start pumping the bait back, moving it far too fast for most of the fish they should be catching. "The slower the retrieve, the better," Fears says. "Drag that bait! Drag it slow and don't move it the entire length of the rod, just a foot or two. Then take up the slack in the line and let the bait sit there for twenty or thirty seconds. Oftentimes the fish are watching the bait, and when they finally decide it's something they can eat, they grab it."

CHECKING YOUR RIG

Fears also advises beginners to check their lines regularly, especially at the point where the weight is attached. "The weight will fray your line, especially if you're using a weight made out of brass," O.T. cautions. "I use a two-bead system, a glass bead and a plastic bead. I place the glass bead on first behind the sinker and then I add the plastic bead, which contains a larger hole. This bead fits over the knot in the line but not over the swivel, so it doesn't allow the glass bead and the weight to come

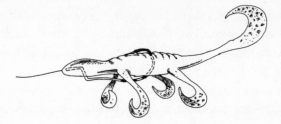

Illustration 9.3 O.T. *likes to expose the hooks by forcing them through the plastic lure, then lightly skin-hooking the point on the opposite side.*

crashing back against your knot. However, this method will fray your line, so check it often."

O.T. also believes that each hook should be, in his words, "texsposed." The Carolina rigger says this means that the point and barb should be pushed all the way through the plastic bait. Then you rest the point on the back of the bait and pull the plastic forward, slipping it over the hook. "This way the point and barb are already exposed when you're ready for the hook-set," Fears says. "You don't have to pull the point through any plastic, and this increases the number of fish you actually catch per bite (Illustration 9.3). Probably the most valuable advice I can give to anglers is to fish the Carolina rig more. To develop confidence in this method, devote a full day to it when conditions are right. Fish the Carolina rig exclusively all day long. By day's end you will be a convert," claims Fears. And his advice to novices just starting their fishing journey: "Pay attention to details. From tying knots, to keeping your hooks sharp, to polishing your casting style, details can make all the difference."

TOO MUCH CONCENTRATION

O.T.'s successes have proved to the world that Carolina rigging for bass fishing will be around for a long time, especially if veterans like Fears continue to make the method famous. O.T.

gets so caught up with Carolina rigging that he sometimes forgets to look at his watch, a trait that can present a problem on the closely monitored time clocks at pro bass tournaments.

"I've been late to a few weigh-ins, which cost me money," Fears admits. He recalls the B.A.S.S. event on the Thousand Island Lake Chain along the St. Lawrence River in New York, which proved to be a costly and humiliating experience. "I probably had enough fish to win already in the livewell," Fears recalls. "But I wanted one big insurance bass. I was concentrating so hard that, in my mind, I convinced myself that my flight of boats was due back to the weigh-in at twenty to four. I was really due back at twenty after three. About three-fifteen it dawned on me, and by the time I got back, with the late penalties, it cost me the tournament."

Despite setbacks like these, O.T. has helped develop many of the techniques that boosted some of his professional peers into the winner's circle. O.T.'s attention to detail in both presentation and bait selection are legendary. Like he says, good fishermen grow out of experience. And O. T. Fears has already accumulated several lifetimes of experience since he left those green hills around Sallisaw and vowed to make a living on the waters he loved.

Robert Hamilton turns to the Sluggo when bass are shallow and
conditions are tough.

10

ROBERT HAMILTON

Why That Sluggo Action Drives Bass Wild

Every year fishing-lure man-ufacturers cross their fin-gers and flood the tackle stores with new baits. Some are gone after a single season. Others endure the test of time and pass from one generation to the next as their ability to coax a bite from a bass becomes legendary.

In the case of the Sluggo, a plastic bait that looks very much like a cross between a slime-coated creature and a banana, success has been synonymous with the rising reputation of Robert Hamilton, an outstanding professional bass angler who started testing wits with Old Bucketmouth not long after he climbed out of diapers. Hamilton, from Jackson, Missis-sippi, began fishing when he was

ROBERT HAMILTON

JACKSON, MISSISSIPPI

1992 BASS Masters Classic Champion. Three-time BASS Masters Classic Finalist.

four years old and was an avid bass angler by the age of seven.

Hamilton's father was also a fisherman, and he took young Robert to area lakes, ponds, and rivers on panfishing expeditions. Soon the young angler developed a passion for bass fishing all on his own. Hamilton acquired a knack for using the baitcast tools of the trade and entered his first official bass competition at fifteen, a tournament that he won. That was the last tournament Hamilton would win, or even participate in, for the next three years. Many of the older bass-club members didn't like the idea of losing to a fifteen-year-old, so they kicked young Robert out of their club and changed the minimum age for membership to eighteen or older.

Yet the slight only served to make the teenager work harder, because the win was like a green light goading him toward a career as a professional fisherman. Hamilton continued to fish with a passion, experimenting with techniques and absorbing and cataloging the details of every angling experience. Soon he was back on the tournament trail and earning the respect of his peers. Today the self-taught angler is a widely respected member of bass fishing's elite, and generally regarded as one of the best Sluggo fishermen in America. And why is the sport so important to Robert Hamilton? "It's the competition with the fish. There are more days they beat us than we beat them," Hamilton explains.

THE SLUGGO: A WORMLIKE BAIT WITH MORE MOVES THAN A HALFBACK

A Sluggo is sort of like a plastic worm, yet fatter, generally shorter, and more angular. The lures truly do look a whole lot like the slugs that leave those silvery trails across your sidewalks on damp nights, thus the name. The angles, or edges of the lure contribute to the famed Sluggo action. Whereas a plastic worm undulates with each twitch of the rod tip, a Sluggo, when fished correctly, reacts more like a falling leaf in the wind, suddenly

Illustration 10.1 *The Sluggo's erratic action is irresistible to bass.*

shooting off at right angles to the line, as if the lure had a life of its own. And that's what drives bass crazy! (Illustration 10.1)

SIGHT OR REACTION BAITS

Hamilton calls them reaction or sight baits. He feels that different baits appeal to the sensory triggers that induce bass to feed—actual sight stimulus, sound or water displacement, or smell. The Mississippi pro relies on Sluggos in situations where bass are feeding by sight, generally in clear or shallow water.

He prefers the original style of Sluggo, because of the bait's famed action. Hamilton likens the movement to that of the legendary Zara Spook, still one of the bass scene's most popular topwater lures after dozens of years on the market. However, unlike the topwater Zara Spook, the Sluggo is fished as a slow-falling bait that is almost always kept in sight. "The initial Sluggo was so porous that the entire lure would twitch back and forth when you worked it," Hamilton points out. "Many of the Sluggo-type lures offered today have a totally different type of action; nothing compares to the old original Sluggo. This is a situational technique; if the conditions are right (bass being shallow), it is a bait that will get you some big bites. You can fish in some pretty heavy cover with the Sluggo. It has an action that most baits can't duplicate."

The Standard Sluggo Retrieve

The Jackson angler says that his standard Sluggo retrieve is a technique called walking the dog. It's the twitch-and-stop style that made the topwater Zara Spook famous: jerk-jerk-pause, jerk-jerk-pause, a motion that remains a favorite among today's best bass fishermen.

Hamilton likes to work the bait in a manner that keeps it in his line of sight. "I just don't think you can react in time if you can't see the fish bite," he says.

The star Sluggo fisherman has another retrieve he turns to at times. "I may pull the lure past a weedbed or stump, kill the action, and let it flutter down," Hamilton says. "Other than that, I just don't have a wide repertoire of retrieves. I generally stick with the jerk-jerk-pause approach, because the key to the bait's success is in the action."

Keying In on Colors

Hamilton feels that lure color does make a difference, but only up to a certain point. "These are clear-water baits, so I depend on natural colors, such as browns and glaze and the shad tones," he says. "If the water is a little bit stained and I'm having dif-ficulty seeing the bait, I may switch to a bubble-gum color.

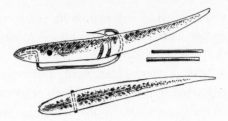

Illustration 10.2 *Bob rigs his Sluggos on a 5/0 offset hook. At times he will insert lead weights to make the lure sink faster. These lead weights look like a nail and can be inserted into the lure crossways at a 90 degree angle and then clipped off even with the side of the Sluggo.*

Sometimes, especially in the spring, you seem to get a few more bites on the bubble-gum shade. But other than that, I don't depend on a lot of colors. Other than the naturals, I only carry about three different colors with me when I fish." Those three include white, clear with a flake added, and the bubble-gum shade. Sometimes Hamilton will substitute a pearl-and-green pattern, but mostly he sticks with those three.

He also likes the bigger sizes, due to the action the bigger baits produce. "When I'm around bedding fish, smallmouth or spotted bass, I may switch to the smaller patterns," Hamilton says. "Generally, though, I'll be throwing the larger sizes."

SLUGGO TACKLE TIPS

He uses a size 5/0, extra-wide gap, extra stiff and stout flipping hook with the bait, usually with lines that range from 10- to 20-pound test (Illustration 10.2). He prefers cone-point hooks, since it takes only three pounds of pressure to penetrate, whereas cutting-edge hooks require six to seven pounds of pressure to bury the hook. The lighter lines are used in clearer water.

His favorite rod is a six-foot, medium-action model, one with a fairly light tip. Hamilton says the softer tip is important. "If your rod is too stiff," he points out, "the fish will blow the bait back if you happen to jerk just as he grabs it. I like a rod with a soft tip yet with plenty of backbone so that I can still bury the hook if I make a long cast."

Hamilton prefers green line, with a low-stretch factor, wound on traditional-style free-spool reels featuring a 5:1 retrieve ratio. Sometimes, with the lighter Sluggo patterns, he'll switch to a spinning reel.

THE STRIKE AND HOOKSET

The Jackson, Mississippi, pro watches his bait closely to detect a strike and then pauses a moment before he sets the hook. "Either I see the fish eat the bait or it just disappears, as if you're looking at it one moment and it's gone the next," Hamilton says. "Then I like to let the fish turn with the bait, pausing just an instant to let the momentum of the bass, as it turns away, actually help me get a good hookset." He says a bass will usually turn either right or left as soon as it closes its mouth around a bait, so a pause brings the hook against the weight of the fish, resulting in very few misses (Illustration 10.3). Hamilton warns beginners, "Remember, don't set the hook too quickly. Many times a bass will come up on this bait and just flash at it, but not actually take it. Make sure the fish has the bait. I work the lure with my rod down and pointed toward the bait. When I jerk it, I move my rod slightly left or right. I also move my arms forward when I see the bite. I'm giving the fish slack so that he doesn't feel any pressure. Many times, if the slightest pressure is felt by a bass, he'll just spit it out. Nobody can react as fast as a bass can spit out a lure. In fact, a bass can spit a bait out and suck it back in three or four times before your brain can react and tell you to set the hook."

WATER AND SPECIAL TECHNIQUES

Hamilton uses Sluggo-type baits in clear water that ranges from approximately 50 degrees up to about 75 degrees. He considers

Illustration 10.3 *Many times you will actually see the bass strike your Sluggo. The bass will almost always turn left or right after taking the lure. It is important to drop your rod tip and allow the fish to move off with the lure before setting the hook.*

the lure to be primarily a spring and fall bait, with exceptions.

One of his favorite exceptions is fishing a Sluggo on a Carolina rig. Hamilton has tested Carolina-rigged Sluggos underwater and videotaped the results. The tapes show what the pro angler suspected: The Sluggos performed on the Carolina rig much the way they do on a regular rig. When a fisherman sweeps with a Sluggo, the bait "walks" behind the rig.

"The key to successful Carolina rigging," Hamilton says, "is the weight." He says that fish key in on the sound the weight makes, the mud it kicks up, or the commotion it causes when it bangs into a rock or underwater log. So, many times the fish are looking down at where the weight is, and the bait passes by unnoticed overhead.

A Sluggo, on the other hand, follows directly behind the weight, tantalizing the bass with its famed side-to-side action.

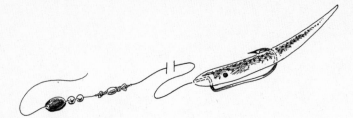

Illustration 10.4 *Bob feels that a Sluggo rigged Carolina style may be the ultimate big bass lure.*

"A Carolina-rigged Sluggo will get you some really big bites," Hamilton points out. "It may not be a bait that will catch you great numbers of fish. But if you need one big bite from one big fish, I don't believe there's a better bait around or a better way to rig it" (Illustration 10.4).

SLUGGO FISHING, WEATHER AND THE SEASONS

The Sluggo pro says that this bait is excellent for prespawn, spawning, and postspawning bass. "You can throw it into the middle of a big school of fry and scatter them, and the males will key in on the bait fast," Hamilton says. He also likes to fish Sluggos in the back of creeks in the fall, when bass move upstream with the schools of shad. In the middle of summer, he uses the bait in early-morning and late-evening situations. In the winter, he says, Sluggos aren't in his bass-fishing arsenal unless they are Carolina-rigged.

Weather conditions have a direct effect on the success or failure of Sluggo baits. "These baits work a lot better in cloudy weather, or windy-weather situations, simply because they are sight baits," Hamilton says. "Fish come up to the surface more when there is cloud cover. In some clear lakes you can draw fish up from fifteen feet to chase the bait. Of course this doesn't mean that Sluggos won't catch fish on bright, sunny days. At times, when the wind is still, I've found Sluggos to be better than spinnerbaits, because fish can see spinnerbaits too clearly when the water is calm."

A Specialized Big-Bite Bait

Hamilton says he chose to concentrate on Sluggos because the bait produces big bites in heavily fished areas. "Sluggos have an action that is very unique," he points out. "It's a natural bait that moves side to side like minnows and eels. I believe Sluggos imitate a lot of natural prey in the food chain. But I had to convince myself."

Hamilton had a bag of Sluggos in his tackle box for a year before he remembered to try the bait. "I guess that just goes to show that when something new comes out, you need to take a look at it. If the lure is totally different, with a totally unique action, odds are the fish are going to bite."

Rigging

Hamilton also urges beginners to get over their fear of casting into heavy cover. "Make sure you rig it exactly straight," he says. "If it's rigged straight, you can fish a Sluggo slowly without a weight. If you want to fish faster, you can add some lead to the middle of the bait, keep it down in the water, and go fast. The clearer the water, the faster I fish; I slow down in dingy water. Plus you can add a few rattles and fish this bait over the tops of weeds and inside grass lines."

Back to the Basics

Hamilton owes his professional success to hard work and attention to the basics. He believes that too many beginning bass fishermen overlook rule one in the pros' mental handbook: Let the fish tell you how to fish for them. Hamilton cautions anglers to "let that first fish you catch tell you what to do and adjust from there. Too many anglers have a tendency to catch a fish and just keep on boating down the bank. When you catch that first fish, note the depth, how it hit the bait, and what kind of cover was nearby. Then fish that area and similar areas thoroughly. If you get a bass in a certain area, there is a physical reason for it, and in most cases more fish will be nearby."

TAKE TECHNIQUES ONE STEP AT A TIME

Hamilton also urges beginners to pick a handful of baits and concentrate on learning how to use them in varying conditions. "Learn what one bait can do before you go on to the next one," he advises. "Stick with basic colors on basic lures. If I had to pick just four, I'd begin with a plastic worm, a Sluggo, a spinnerbait, and a crankbait. You'll be able to catch fish at some spot on any lake with those four lures, and do it at any time of the year. Don't take anything for granted. Look after every detail of your tackle, lures, and retrieve."

Robert learned his lesson about taking things for granted in a big-money team bass tournament. He and a friend were fishing on Ross Barnett Reservoir in Mississippi. "I considered this lake my home territory," Robert explains. "My partner and I knew this area like the back of our hand, and we had two five-fish limits of big fish before noon. We were so sure that we had won that we napped in the shade for a couple of hours and then boated around the lake looking for new spots, eating cookies, and gloating over our good fortune while we waited for three o'clock to weigh-in. At weigh-in time, not only did we not win, but we finished third, just ounces out of first place. If we had continued to fish and had caught just one more bass that was larger than one of the ones we weighed in, we could have released the smaller fish, kept the larger fish, and won. This lesson cost us several thousand dollars."

WINNING THE BIG ONE

Hamilton says the most unforgettable moment of his fishing career came when he won the BASS Masters Classic Tournament. "I practiced with the locals for a couple of days to find all the secret places on the lake, only to discover that everybody was fishing those secret places," he remembers. That's when Hamilton took all the fishing tackle out of his boat, grabbed a topo map, turned on the depth finder, and went on an idling expedition. He cruised around the water for two more days, determined to find some secret places of his own. "I found maybe fifty spots that I thought had potential for when we came back a month later," he recalls. "Then I got my rods out and eliminated some more."

Then, during the actual competition, Hamilton's search paid off. "I was in a position to go ahead, but to actually win the thing, I needed to get on some fish that weren't spooked," he said. "There was a tremendous amount of spectator-boat traffic and it was pushing the shad down onto the deeper humps, so I fished deeper and got some really good bites."

Later, after he'd won the tournament, Hamilton's fellow pros congratulated him for realizing that the spectator boats would raise havoc with the shallow fish. That recognition, he says, was almost as sweet as the check. It seems that a large part of this bass-fishing game remains the mental duel as much as the winning, even if you are a BASS Masters Classic Champion, and one who notched his first tournament win at an age when most boys begin to shave.

TRICKS OF THE TRADE
25 Pros and 50 Tips

———————

1. • HANK PARKER

Spool and Line

Obviously the best way to spool new line on your free-spool reel is with a partner holding the spool of line so that it can spin easily with moderate resistance. If you don't have someone to help you, here are some tips to spool line yourself. First, for a bulk reel of spool it's a good idea to get a clean trash can, put the spool in the can, and let the spool bounce around as you wind it in. If you are on the lake, a good tip is to take your large bulk spool, attach it to the reel, run it through the guides, and throw the spool in the lake and reel it in. The water will create tension to get more consistent line coverage on your reel. Make sure you retrieve the excess line and spool from the water, as the line is not biodegradable and can tangle in props and will harm wildlife.

Hook Setting

The most efficient way to set a hook is not by muscling the rod quickly into your body but by generating rod-tip speed. Think of it as cracking a whip. Once you feel the bass, pick up the bait and drop the rod tip down, get a slight amount of slack in the line, and just whip that rod tip upward. You will find this tip will improve your hook-setting ratio.

2. • GEORGE COCHRAN

Weather and Water Conditions

Always pay attention to the weather and water conditions on a lake. If the water is coming up on a lake, the fish will be shallow. If the water is dropping, the fish will move to the channel or the first drop-off from the shallow water. If the weather is cloudy or rainy, the fish are shallow and are usually biting good. If the sun is out, the fish are usually tight to cover and tight to drop-offs, and you have to fish slower.

Changing Bait Colors

In my thirty-plus years of fishing, one thing I have learned that helps me catch more fish is changing the color of baits until you find the best color for that day. Also, after you have found some fish, change lures to help you catch a few more fish in the same area. An example of this is if you were catching fish on a chartreuse spinnerbait and the fish in an area stop biting, put on a chartreuse crankbait and again fish the same area.

3. • JAY YELAS

Fishing Shallow Shoreline Cover

Very few anglers will fish with a crankbait when working shallow shoreline cover. Most use spinnerbaits. Try a Storm Short Wart in these shallow-cover situations. Bass grow weary of seeing spinnerbaits all the time, and giving them a different look with a Short Wart is often the key to success. You can even follow a spinnerbait fisherman down a bank and catch fish behind him with this method.

Braided Line

Since none of the new braided lines are round, knots tied in braided line have a tendency to slip and break. To ensure that this does not happen, use a drop of fishing glue on your knot and you should not have this problem.

4. • DENNY BRAUER

Lure Color*

How do you know which color of lure to choose on any given day? Here are some shortcuts I use that work well.

On cloudy days, darker colors seem to work better. On bright, sunny days, lighter, more subtle colors, seem to work best. Also let the water color help dictate lure selection. In stained or muddy water, I have my best luck with bright fluorescent colors. In clear water, natural or translucent colors often work best. Examples would be: a chartreuse spinnerbait in dirty water and a white one in clear water.

I also prefer lighter-color lures for topwater or mid-depth, and dark lures when fishing deep or near the bottom. Sound lures are good when the water is stained. In very clear water, it often helps to go to a smaller lure or shorter worm.

Sneak Attack*

With more and more people taking to the waterways, the popularity of fishing boats, pleasure boats, skiers, and jet skis has increased, not to mention the daily occurrence of commercial vessels. Consequently, fish have gotten acclimated to any number of sounds produced on the water by man. This only serves to make the fish more aware of what is going on around them.

Approach your fishing as slowly and quietly as possible. Scout your fishing area so that you do not have to run over it multiple times to try to locate your honey hole. Use your trolling motor in place of your outboard. Avoid loud noises in your boat. For example avoid dropping things such as anchors, tackle

*Asterisked material is compliments of Humminbird.

boxes, and drink cans. You can up your chances of catching fish if you practice a subtle approach.

5. • LONNIE STANLEY

Jigs and Pork Rind

Since most bait fish and crawfish are lighter in color on their underneath side, I always turn the lighter-colored fat side of my pork-rind bait down when fishing a jig. Also, a bass can feel the soft fat side better on the bottom side of its mouth, which in turn will make it hold on longer.

Natural Baits

I like to keep my baits looking natural. This one thing has really helped my bass fishing. I like to use color-coded worm weights while fishing a worm or lizard. For example, using a black/red flake worm, I would coordinate with a black, or black/red flake worm weight. Another example would be a purple worm with a purple weight. Keeping it looking natural will help your fishing. I have never seen a shiny-headed worm or lizard swim by my boat.

6. • BERNIE SCHULTZ

Spinnerbaits in Clear Water

In spite of what many anglers believe, spinnerbaits can work in clear water. By considering their cosmetics and utilizing some basic retrieves, you will find spinnerbaits can make great clear-water tools.

The single most important factor in spinnerbait fishing is wind. Without it the pattern will usually fail. With it you can have a feeding frenzy.

Next, try to match the available forage with blade size and skirt colors. A good key is either to match the blade profile with the overall body size of the baitfish or to match the jig portion to the head size of the baitfish. Fish feeding in clear water are usually triggered by sight. Make sure your components (skirts, blades) are as believable as possible. Subtle colors are usually best, not bright.

The last thing to remember is to keep the bait above the fish's head. Slower retrieves give bass the opportunity to refuse the bait. A faster, over-the-head presentation will result in more impulse strikes. It's not necessary to "wake" the lure, but keep the retrieve brisk and over the fish.

Protecting the Resource

Many anglers have gotten so caught up in learning how to catch more fish, they sometimes forget the tremendous responsibility they have to the future of the sport. Although our environmental problems are vast, one area we can all help in is preventing littering. Litter is one of the most visible and depressing problems I see when I fish on lakes and rivers across the country.

You can do your part to improve fishing, and the beauty of our water, by never throwing anything overboard, including the most insignificant or smallest of items. Try to make the lake cleaner than when you arrived. My boat compartments look like trash bins at the end of the day because I pick up so much trash as I go along. I do it because it makes me feel better, makes the lake look better, and ensures for future generations a clean environment in which to catch fish. Leave the lake in better shape than you found it!

7. • PENNY BERRYMAN

Lure Testing*

Lures such as crankbaits usually run better and certainly deeper when fishing with light line. But if you really want to learn how your lures perform, take them to a local swimming pool for testing. If the pool has depths up to nine or ten feet, you will be able to monitor the performance on various outfits as well as line sizes. You'll discover which lures have a slow versus fast wobble, which ones suspend, and how quickly some baits reach their maximum depths.

Skip a Rat*

Here's a trick to try in the middle of the day at the time of year when the topwater bite is strong. Find a bank that has thick branches, heavy brush, or willow trees hanging over the water— one that is extremely difficult to cast, flip, or pitch into. Select a snag-free Mann's Rat or Ghost, tie it on 17- or 20-pound test, rigged on a heavy-duty spincast reel, such as a Zebco 808. With a little practice, you will be able to skip the lure underneath everything that seems impenetrable.

The line will feed off the spincast reel and the lure will bounce and skip its way into the heaviest of obstacles. You will not experience a backlash with this rig. Be ready for some vicious strikes, because fish in this environment haven't seen many lures. I prefer a 5½- to 6-foot, medium- to heavy-action graphite rod for this type of brush bustin'.

8. • WOO DAVES

Distance and Small Spinnerbaits

I use a lot of ⅛-ounce spinnerbaits. Because of their small frame, they work well in clear water. Sometimes, though, with the small lure you can't get the distance you need on a cast, so I take a ⅛- to ¼-ounce split shot and crimp it right behind the skirt. This will give me the weight I need to get the distance while still enabling me to keep the lure frame small.

Tough Fishing

When fishing really gets tough, one lure I can almost always catch a few fish on is a #2 Mepps spinner. This is overlooked by other pros. This little spinner usually works well in clear or stained water. Its in-line design gives it a different look.

Breakline Fishing*

One of the least-talked-about and best-kept secrets of the pro anglers is breakline fishing. Fishing a break, usually the first or second change of depth or edge of underwater grass, either inside edge or outside edge, is a proven tournament winner.

So many fishermen simply fish down a shoreline without paying attention to the changes of depth that occur down this run. By paying attention to your depth finder you can easily follow the contour as it changes from deep to shallow. Ten feet of water might be ten yards from the shoreline at one spot and forty yards out at another.

Don't worry about the shoreline, but instead let your depth finder guide you to success by following the breakline.

9. • TOM MANN, JR.

Pegging a Doodle Worm

When you are doodlin' worms in deep water, and you want to peg your worm to the eye of your hook, take a short piece of 30- or 40-pound monofilament line and place it through the worm and eye instead of a toothpick. This will keep the worm up on your hook and allow you to set the hook better.

More Spinnerbait Vibration

When you are fishing a willowleaf blade on a spinnerbait and you would like a little more vibration, try the following: Just take a pair of needle-nose pliers and bend the last ⅛ inch in about 90 degrees toward the concave side of the blade. This will give you much more vibration.

10. • JIMMY HOUSTON

*Organize for Better Success**

You can maximize your success as an angler by simply being organized. Keep your boat arranged so you know where your necessary items are located. Devise a system whereby your lures are separated by type and application. So when conditions change, you can do so without hunting high and low for your equipment.

A tackle storage system helps a lot. Tackle boxes are designed to use interchangeable small boxes which can be adjusted for each trip. Mark these boxes on the end so they can be readily identified. At the beginning of each season, clean and reorganize each box. Replace old skirts, rusted hooks and discolored worms.

Feeling better about how your tackle is arranged will help your overall fishing attitude.

Grassbeds on a Drop-off

When fishing grassbeds that go from shallow water and then drop off into a channel or just deeper water, position your boat in the deeper water and cast a spinnerbait. Cast the spinnerbait out over the weedbed and retrieve it back, letting it just "tick" the tops of the weedbeds. When the bait gets to the drop-off, let the spinnerbait helicopter straight down the drop-off. Strip line off your reel as the spinnerbait drops so that the spinnerbait will helicopter *straight* down. *Watch your line* as the bait drops. When the bass bites, the line will jump or the line will "straighten," giving you indication of a bite. Set the hook and try to turn the bass's head so that he won't waller back into the weeds.

11. • LARRY NIXON

Open-Faced Reels and Line

If you are a user of open-faced fishing reels, try this trick. The night before you go fishing, soak your spool in a glass of water. The next day your line will be limp and fish just like new line. No more line jumping off the spool when you cast.

Jig and Pork Tip

When using a jig with a pork, slide a small piece of plastic worm (approximately ¼ inch) on the hook shank. This will keep the pork from sliding up and getting in front of the hook point. If you use a piece of a chartreuse worm, it will add extra color, which sometimes makes a big difference.

12. • DICK HEALEY

Catching "Double" Bass

With just a little understanding of fish behavior, fishermen can catch "doubles" quite often. Fish, like other animals, are competitive. We know that bass are not particularly solitary predators, because they generally hunt in groups and remain together as a gregarious species. But when a bass successfully attacks a prey, other bass in the area become very excited. They look for similar prey and even attempt to steal the original prey.

You may have observed this behavior in chickens. When a chicken picks up a food morsel that isn't swallowed immediately, he is literally chased around the pen by other chickens trying to take it away from him or to find more of the same.

So, how do you catch "doubles"? When you get a hit or a pickup, have your fishing partner cast to that location just as you set the hook. Quite often, he will instantly catch a second fish. This technique is extremely effective with plastic worms.

But if you plan to use this trick, be prepared to swallow your ego, because that second fish will probably be larger than the first.

13. • O. T. FEARS

Modifying a Jig

Most fishermen take a jig out of the package and use it. That's fine, because a jig is one of the best bass baits there is. However, there are some adjustments that can be made to catch a few more fish and to keep from hanging up so much.

Most jigs come with too much skirt material. Hold the jig by the head with the skirt hanging down. Take some scissors and cut the excess rubber just below the bottom of the hook, approximately ⅛ to ¼ inch. This allows bass to see your trailer better and prevents them from grabbing just the back of the skirt.

To increase the weedlessness, divide the weedguard fibers in half. Place your thumb between and push down, spreading the bristles to the right and left of the hook point. This will keep the jig from rolling on its side and hanging so easily.

Advantages of Using a Snap

For all crankbaits, topwater lures, and jerkbaits, I use a snap to attach the lure to my line. The advantages of this type of attachment are: increased lure action, ease of changing lures quickly, and knot stability. The snap allows the lure to swing freely from side to side, maximizing any action the lure was designed to have. The lure can be changed quickly without having to retie each time. Tying the line to a split ring doesn't give very good results due to the shape of the ring. Split rings are not round and have two sharp ends, which can cut your line. These factors make tying to a snap better.

14. • KEN COOK

A Tip on How Deep to Start Fishing*

If a bass fisherman can learn the depth at which fish are holding, he can usually figure out how to catch them. Here's a simple way to determine how deep to start fishing.

Lower a white object, such as a spinnerbait, into the water until it disappears. This distance will be equal to one-half the light-penetration depth. And since bass like to remain in shaded areas whenever possible, you will normally find them at depths between where the white disappears and twice that depth.

Heavily stained water can often drive bass shallow, while extremely clear water will send them down. In clear water, always fish the shaded side of the structure. Make longer casts with lighter line and lures to avoid spooking the fish.

Water Temperature Trend

In the springtime the key thing is temperature. This is because the bass is a very cold-blooded animal and temperature is very important to their activity level. The warmer the water, the more active the bass. The temperature of the water is important, but the trend of the water temperature may be more important. This is relevant in the lower end of the fish-catching zone, such as temperatures in the lower fifties and high forties. Whether the temperature is higher or lower than it was yesterday seems to determine how easy the bass will be to catch. For example, you go out there and catch bass on one day and the water temperature is 52 degrees. The water temperature warms to 55 the next day, and then a cold front moves in and the water temperature drops back to 52 degrees. Fishing won't be nearly as good as it was two days before when the water temperature was 52 degrees. Two days before, the trend was a water temperature increase, and now the trend is a water temperature decrease. This is what I mean by looking at the water temperature trend. You need to see what the water temperature has been in the past couple of days. This will tell you how well the fish will be biting.

15. • JOE THOMAS

Cold, Muddy Water Conditions

Under cold, muddy water conditions, try using a lightweight quarter-ounce rubber jig with an oversized trailer, such as a #3 Uncle Josh Pork Frog. This light-jig/big-frog combo allows the bait to fall slowly yet displace a lot of water, which is critical in muddy water. Black on Black is usually the hot color.

Another Muddy Water Tip

Worm and jig rattles can be very effective under muddy-water conditions or dark conditions (such as fishing through matted vegetation). The rattle tends to call the fish from greater distances.

16. • RICH TAUBER

Clear Water Topwater Fishing

When you grow up on clear water, you learn how to fish it. Early in the year I like to use a topwater minnow lure, such as a Rebel, with a black back and silver sides. I try to make long casts to cover what I can see in the water. Look for shady spots in the water. The long cast is the key. The fish has great vision in clear water, so stay back. The clear water works to your advantage because the fish can see the lure hit. Let it rest and then twitch it with short, quick movements. After ten or so twitches, reel it back, staying alert for a strike. In summer and on into fall, the Zara Spook, which has a fantastic side-to-side action when you learn to work it, will catch fish consistently. Work the lure close to cover and stay with it.

Fishing for Bedding Bass

When fishing bedding bass or bass that you see roaming in shallow water, try to keep still. By staying still in the boat and keeping movement to a minimum, you will become part of the environment to the fish and the fish will become more at ease. Try to watch the fish and notice if the fish has any particular habits. Does it protect certain areas, swim in certain cycles, and so on? Stay still and make repeated casts to the fish and don't give up. Fish in shallow water can be caught. Just take your time and be patient.

Green Line in Clear Water

Try to use more green line in clear-water situations, and on all reaction baits. I like green Stren line. I have noticed a marked increase in the number of strikes I get with green line in clear water.

17. • BILL DANCE

Catch and Release[†]

Released fish represent angling tomorrows. Releasing a fish seems simple enough: Unhook 'em and toss 'em back. Unfortunately, it isn't that easy. All fish have a protective coating over their bodies to guard against bacterial infection. Removing a part of that coating lowers the fish's resistance to diseases. Have a wet hand if you touch the fish. Grasping small fish tightly during unhooking can cause internal damage to the fish. Netting can also harm the fish by removing some of its mucous coating and scales. Loose or open hooks on a lure can catch in a net's mesh, tearing the fish's mouth or soft tissues. Don't allow a fish to flop on the boat floor or on the ground. Release smaller fish without removing them from the water. Hold the rod-tip

[†]Daggered material is compliments of Mercury.

high and grasp the hook with a pair of fishing pliers. Deeply hooked fish have a greater chance of survival if the hook is left in and the line is clipped off close to the eye.

Being Observant

Without question, paying close attention to what you're doing, and what's going on around you while fishing, will definitely make you a much better fisherman. If you persist in worrying about what happened at work, or whether the yard needs mowing, or what you've got to do next week, or something else, you might as well load up and pick another day to fish.

Fishing should be fun, and you should be out there enjoying yourself, not worrying about something else. Your concentration should be on your fishing. Concentrating on what's taking place around you can tip the scales toward success. You've got to recognize a set of circumstances and then take advantage of them.

A good angler hears as well as sees, and his mind registers the impressions. If, for example, a bass busts a baitfish on the surface behind you, your ears should convey the message, even though you are concentrating on casting on a target. The trick is to train your senses to accept the commonplace in nature and seek out the unusual.

18. • ROLAND MARTIN

Log Your Bass Catch[†]

Keep a log of every bass you catch this coming year. List all of the conditions: location (structure), cover, depth, bottom consistency, water temperature, water clarity, pH, oxygen, wind speed and direction, sunlight conditions, moon phase, season, and date. You will be writing your own fishing diary. Next year, when you return to that lake, you will have advance information on at least where to start.

19. • ZELL ROWLAND

Check the Guides on Your Rod

One of the fastest ways to lose the biggest bass of your life is to fail to check the guides on your rod. Most have ceramic inserts, which is a great innovation. However, these guides take a terrific beating. After having had line running through them for hours and being used as a pry pole to push and pull baits loose from snags, a bad guide can cut your line like a knife. The best way to check your guides is to take a Q-Tip swab and run it around the inside of each guide. If one has a nick, the swab will hang up and leave cotton in the guide, on the nick or cut.

Patterns Within a Pattern*

An example of pattern fishing would be catching a bass off a stump, then finding another stump and catching another bass. Patterns can be developed around lures, fishing locations, structure configurations, and a number of other conditions.

The key to real success is finding a pattern within a pattern. Pay attention to such details as the following: Was the bass you caught on the sunny side of the stump? Was it on the windy side, the down-current side, the shallow side, etc. Note the bottom texture. Was it hard clay, soft mud, pea gravel? Did the water have some stain? Observe what the fish is trying to tell you. Patterns within patterns can be the key to your angling success. Water temperature is also important. Note it when you catch a fish.

20. • RICK CLUNN

Glass Rods†

When using fast-moving lures, such as crankbaits or spinnerbaits, I still prefer to use a glass or glass-tip rod rather than a graphite or other high-tech-material rod. I feel I hook fish better on the glass rods and consequently don't lose as many. A bass inhales a lure instead of striking it. In order for the fish to inhale the fast-moving lure on a tight line, something must give it to him. A glass-tip rod will flex toward the fish and, having slower flex-recovery time, allows the fish to inhale the bait deeper. In addition, the glass or glass-tip rod is not as sensitive as high-tech materials, so the fisherman allows the fish to have the lure before he jerks to set the hook.

21. • FREDDA LEE

Matching Bait Fish Colors

In clear water, pay special attention to the forage or baitfish the bass are feeding on. The colors of the forage will change subtly with the seasonal patterns, water clarity, and light penetration. Choose your topwater lures and crankbaits to match these color variations in order to give your lures a more natural appearance.

Create a Filing System for Maps and Info

I like to use large, tearproof envelopes, labeling each one with a waterproof marker, and store them all in a small file cabinet or cardboard file box. I keep all my records on each lake together; guide cards, motel and travel brochures, photo files, logbooks, and so on. File each set of maps and info alphabetically. You'll find all you need to know in one neat, simple package.

22. • GUY EAKER

What Spinnerbait to Use*

Spinnerbaits have become one of the bass fisherman's most popular and versatile lures. But why are some anglers consistently more successful with a spinnerbait than others? Perhaps it is because they know what size, color, and blade combinations to use under different conditions. Here are some guidelines.

When bass are feeding on one- to two-inch baitfish, I'll use a ⅛- or ¼-ounce spinnerbait for best results. When the baitfish are between three and five inches, I'll throw a ⅜- to ¾-ounce lure. I select willowleaf blades when the bass are feeding and aggressive. But when the water is cold or the bass are not moving or feeding, I'll use Colorado- or Indiana-style blades.

Controlling Crankbait Depth

When using different-size lines, always remember that to get a crankbait to run deep, use small line. To get a crankbait to run shallow, use big line. When I won the B.A.S.S. tournament at Sam Rayburn, Texas, I used 16- and 20-pound Magna Thin line. It helped me to fish the crankbait a lot slower over four and five feet of grass and to tick the top of the grass. This is what helped me win the tournament.

Boat Dock Strategy*

If there is one bass-locating strategy that has always paid off for me, it's fishing boat docks. No matter where I fish, whether in a new impoundment or in an old familiar lake, boat docks have always been a surefire producer.

Boat docks provide the same cover as natural structure. Plus, many dock owners conveniently sink or bury brush and trees in and around their docks to provide fish habitat. During winter drawdown, scout as many boat docks as you can. Take photos and make notes of the structure-ladened docks. Plus, look for the telltale signs: Rod holders, minnow buckets, and lights positioned over the water means it's a fishing dock.

23. • TOMMY MARTIN

Being Versatile

In my opinion, to catch bass consistently, you must know how to use all the different bass-fishing techniques and lures. One ingredient all top tournament anglers have is that they are versatile. As we compete in tournaments, on lakes across the United States, there is a time for flipping. The time for flipping is when the water level is high and there is cover in the water. However, if the lake is low and there's no cover in the water, dragging a Carolina rig just may be the best bet. A good bass fisherman must know how to do it all; flip, pitch, worm-fish, jig-fish, spinnerbait-, crankbait-, topwater- and finesse-fish. Let the lake conditions, the season, and the weather dictate your approach to bass fishing.

Experimenting with Speed of Retrieve

An angler must be willing to experiment with his speed of retrieve if he expects to catch bass consistently. When you are crankbaiting, spinnerbaiting, fishing a Texas-rigged worm or a Carolina lizard or a craw, you must find out how fast the bass want the bait moved. As a rule of thumb, when the water is stained, or muddy and colder, you will have to move your lures from very slowly to a medium-speed retrieve. However, on the other hand, when the water is clear, even if it is cold, there are times that bass want crankbaits and spinnerbaits moved fast. Usually, right after a cold front in the spring, even in clear water, you will need to slow way down with your Texas-rigged worm or Carolina rig.

24. • TERRY BAKSAY

Fish Hunting

Use a bright-colored Sluggo (bubble gum, banana, Merthiolate, or chartreuse/pepper) as a search bait to find and locate fish. Bass are as curious as cats and will move out of cover to see what that bright-colored "thing" is. Then you can either catch them with a Sluggo or use a jig or a worm to catch a fish you otherwise might not have caught. I call this the pointer method of fish hunting.

Customizing Spinning Rod Handles

One trick I use to customize my spinning equipment is to use rods with Tennessee-type handles. I use electrical tape to attach my reel to the rod, and then on top of that I get tennis racket handle–grip tape and put that over the electrical tape. My purpose in using the grip tape is to make the grip softer, warmer in cold weather, and more comfortable overall.

25. • CHARLIE CAMPBELL

Take Care of Your Equipment

There's an old saying that goes, "You take care of your equipment and it will take care of you." This certainly applies to your boat, motor, and trailer. A little periodic maintenance will pay dividends when the fish are on the line.

Occasionally, pull the prop from both the outboard as well as the trolling motor. Discarded monofilament has a tendency to wrap around the prop shafts. Remove this potential problem. Keep the bearing greased on your trailer. Every month or so shoot a little grease into the hubs, especially during a period of heavy trailering.

When dust and grime are apparent on the boat's surface, a shot of furniture polish and a soft cloth can restore the luster temporarily. Check battery terminals and remove corrosive buildup with an old toothbrush and a bit of baking soda.

A Little Topwater Tip

When you are topwater fishing, there is a tendency to set the hook when you see the fish strike. *Never* set the hook until you feel the fish on the line. This tip will keep you from losing fish when you are topwater fishing.